WE WILL SECURE OUR FUTURE

Portrait of Peterson Zah

We Will Secure
Our Future

Empowering the Navajo Nation

PETERSON ZAH AND
PETER IVERSON

THE UNIVERSITY OF
ARIZONA PRESS
TUCSON

THE UNIVERSITY OF
ARIZONA PRESS

© 2012 The Arizona Board of Regents
All rights reserved

www.uapress.arizona.edu

Library of Congress Cataloging-in-Publication Data
Zah, Peterson.
 We will secure our future : empowering the Navajo nation / Peterson Zah and
Peter Iverson.
 p. cm.
 Includes bibliographical references and index.
 ISBN 978-0-8165-0246-2 (cloth : alk. paper) — ISBN 978-0-8165-0247-9
(pbk. : alk. paper) 1. Navajo Nation, Arizona, New Mexico & Utah—History.
2. Navajo Indians—Social conditions. 3. Navajo Indians—Economic conditions.
4. Navajo Indians—Politics and government. 5. Self-determination, National—
Southwest, New. I. Iverson, Peter. II. Title.
 E99.N3Z34 2012
 979.1004'9726—dc23
 2011045474

Manufactured in the United States of America on acid-free, archival-quality paper
containing a minimum of 30% post-consumer waste and processed chlorine free.

17 16 15 14 13 12 6 5 4 3 2 1

To Ros and our three children, Elaine, Eileen,
and Keeyonnie, and our grandchildren
—PZ

To Kaaren
—PI

Contents

Illustrations

Preface

PETERSON ZAH

I BELIEVE IN THE BEAUTY AND THE VALUE of oral tradition so much that I hesitate translating my beliefs of Diné history, culture, and customs to English. Oral tradition when translated no longer has the impact of our Navajo language; rather, the integrity of Diné values is given to a pen. The stories, values, and traditions are supposed to be heard. Once written, oral tradition becomes compromised and stationary; it is no longer alive. Missing is the much-needed dialogue for a complete understanding. Despite my personal views, I see the composition of the Navajo population changing. Therefore, I feel the responsibility to share my memories for future generations. Unfortunately, it is in written form.

My life has encompassed many roles: teacher, VISTA program coordinator, DNA People's Legal Services director, executive director of the Southwest Indian Development, Inc., Window Rock School Board member, Navajo Nation chairman/president, Save the Children regional director, and multiple roles at Arizona State University. Growing up I was taught the important value of helping one another. I see this teaching reflected in my life's work. In retirement, my hope is that the young Navajo people today will not abandon the value of helping and will continue to honor our traditions.

When I was a child, we played with *hashtlish* (clay) from mountain springs. With hashtlish we formed animals and people and were able to give each of our creations the best qualities, much in the way families try to mold and shape their children. I would like to express my gratitude to the people of my clans—the Kiiyaa'áanii, Táchii'nii, Tódich'íí'nii, and Tótsohnii people who all helped form me—in

particular, my late mother Mae Multine Zah and my late dad Henry Zah. We lost my mother in May 2010. My mother was an extraordinary teacher, weaver, and carrier of tradition. She taught me to be caring, generous, and appreciative of all that life has to offer. I am grateful to my wife, Rosalind, and her family, the Honágháahni and Naakaii Diné, who have actively supported and taken care of me. Additionally, I express much appreciation to the many, many colleagues and friends I have come into contact with throughout the years. Their dedication and commitment have served not only the Navajo people but also many others.

The pages that follow portray a glimpse of my life. I don't consider myself an extraordinary Navajo person, rather a Navajo person who had extraordinary experiences. *Ahéhee'*.

Preface

PETER IVERSON

THIS IS A BOOK CENTERED ON THE LIFE and career of Peterson Zah. From 1986 to 2010, I taught American Indian history and Navajo history at Arizona State University (ASU). During this time I invited many individuals to speak to my classes. No one had a stronger impact upon my students than Mr. Zah. Through the stories he told about his own experiences and the evolution of the Navajo Nation, he illustrated the ability of indigenous groups to make changes on their own terms and to continue as distinctive, viable communities.

Born in Keams Canyon, Arizona, in 1937, Peterson Zah has long been a major figure in Navajo and Southwestern life. He has exemplified the determination of Indian people to gain greater control over their lives and lands. Zah became well known throughout the Navajo Nation and the surrounding region as the director of the Navajo Legal Services program. The Navajos later elected him as chairman of the Navajo Tribal Council and as president of the Navajo Nation. Zah also served as a special advisor to Lattie Coor and Michael Crow, presidents of ASU, in regard to American Indian issues and concerns. He played a crucial role in dramatically improving ASU's record in regard to the enrollment, retention, and graduation of Indian students.

I knew a book on Peterson Zah's own remarkable story would have wide appeal, but I also knew it would never be published unless I or someone else intervened. Mr. Zah had taken on too many responsibilities. However, he did agree to meet with me for a few hours every three months or so to record his memories and

xiii

reflections about his own life and career and the Navajo past, present, and future.

I have edited slightly portions of our observations while maintaining our distinctive voices. Unedited copies of these sessions have been transcribed and will be available, together with CD copies, at the Labriola National American Indian Data Center, Arizona State University Libraries.

As do many Navajo stories, this book includes a circle or two. Peterson Zah graduated from ASU in 1963 with a degree in education. At that time, few Indian students enrolled at the university and even fewer completed their programs. It gave him great satisfaction to return to Tempe and find ways to make it possible for a much higher number of students to reach the finish line.

If he could circle back to Tempe, he could also circle back to Window Rock. In November 2010, just before celebrating his 73rd birthday, he resigned his position at ASU and went back home to Window Rock. For some time he had been anxious about the growing Navajo political turmoil centered there. Zah helped establish a new organization whose name strongly suggests what its members hoped to achieve. It is called Restore Harmony (http://www .restoreharmony.net/). Its website declared the group would "focus our efforts toward the future and visualize a positive change on the Navajo Nation." As a brief epilogue suggests, Peterson Zah's involvement in Restore Harmony promised to be another fascinating chapter in his life and career.

This book is divided into eight overlapping chapters: Generations, Schools, Leaders, Lawyers, Traders, Neighbors, Resources, and Tomorrows. Each chapter begins with a quotation by Zah taken from a longer passage in that section of the book. I offer a brief contextual essay at the start of each chapter. I provide a concise list of volumes for further reading for each chapter at the end of the book. In addition to books relating to Navajo history and culture, there also are listed some with relevant national or regional perspectives.

I met Peterson Zah during my first year in Navajo country. I had accepted a last-minute invitation to join the faculty of Navajo Community College (now Diné College). Members of my family have known members of his family since the mid-1930s, when my

mother's father became the principal of the federal Indian school at Fort Wingate, New Mexico, just outside of Gallup. Kenneth Begay and Eleanor Bryant (who eventually became Mr. Zah's father-in-law and mother-in-law) numbered among the students at the school at that time. My grandfather would have happily remained at Wingate, but the federal search for a replacement for the principal at Keams Canyon prompted his somewhat involuntary transfer northward. He was living in that community, then, when Peterson Zah was born there in 1937.

My grandparents moved to Whittier, California, following my grandfather's retirement. I drove over to see them in the autumn of 1969. After a wonderful weekend, during which I began to realize additional connections between my grandparents' time and my own, I returned to Navajo Community College armed with copies of the Wingate yearbooks from the 1930s. Kenneth Begay had gone on to become one of the truly great silversmiths of the Southwest. In 1969, he and I became colleagues on the Navajo Community College faculty. When confronted with one of those high school yearbook photographs we'd prefer never to see again, he seemed other than overjoyed. I can still hear his voice. "Where did you get that?" he asked. Other connections have followed through the years, including the beautiful wedding rings crafted for Kaaren and me by another master silversmith, Harvey Begay (Kenneth and Eleanor Begay's son).

If my grandparents helped inspire my specific interest in Navajo country, many other family members also encouraged my interest in stories, place, and memory. Kaaren's participation in this project made this book possible. Her love, patience, strength, and grace continue to make better each of my days.

It has been an honor to work with Peterson Zah on this book. Throughout his career he has sought to enable Navajos at the individual, community, and national level to gain greater control over their lives and lands. He has never manipulated the public trust for private gain. His actions have been informed by two concepts: *hozho* and *k'é*, which address the importance of recognizing and taking care of kinship obligations through acts that reflect generosity and kindness and result in harmony and beauty. In that spirit, Zah has

consistently attempted to build bridges rather than construct walls. He has always recognized there is no substitute for hard work or, for that matter, a sense of humor.

Peterson Zah has never asked for special consideration or relied on tired excuses when things did not go exactly as he might have desired. Recognizing the world is not always just or fair, he will frequently observe, "Don't call it a problem, call it a challenge. Let's see what we can do about it."

Acknowledgments

ARCHIVISTS AND OTHER STAFF MEMBERS of various libraries contributed in an important way to this book. Joyce Martin and Pat Etter of the Labriola National American Indian Data Center at Hayden Library, Arizona State University, furnished significant support for this project from beginning to end. The Labriola Center offered us an ideal setting for interviews touching upon many vital subjects. Joyce Martin arranged for the recording and transcription of these sessions. Rob Spindler, the head of Special Collections at Hayden Library, together with Eunice Kahn, archivist of the Navajo Nation Museum, allowed us to employ some wonderful photographs by Milton Snow. Staff members at Special Collections of Cline Library at Northern Arizona University also helped us locate additional valuable photographs. We also thank the Office of the President at Arizona State University for its financial assistance that made the inclusion of these photographs possible.

WE WILL SECURE OUR FUTURE

Introduction

PETER IVERSON

PETERSON ZAH'S LIFE AND CAREER have reflected the determination of indigenous individuals to be members of viable Indian communities as well as citizens of the United States. Zah rose to prominence as director of the Navajo Legal Services program and then went on to serve as chairman of the Navajo Tribal Council and as president of the Navajo Nation. He also played a vital role within Arizona State University (ASU) as a special advisor to the ASU president in regard to American Indian issues and concerns. Working with other Indian staff and faculty, he helped raise dramatically the enrollment, retention, and graduation of Native students. In recognition of these and other achievements, in 2005 the university awarded him an honorary doctorate.

This essay provides historical context for a more thorough understanding of and appreciation for Peterson Zah's life and career. It examines three eras, noting some of the reasons why these periods have mattered. In each of these times, the Navajos faced concerted efforts by outsiders who sought to exploit their resources as well as limit their options and assimilate them into a larger society. Yet the Navajos showed they could do what they needed to do to bolster and maintain a degree of separation and sovereignty. Through the actions of individuals, families, and communities, the Navajos rejected the idea they were a vanishing people.

The first period began with the arrival of Spanish colonists in the Southwest in the sixteenth and seventeenth centuries. The livestock brought by the Spanish transformed Navajo life. Sheep, horses, goats, and cattle became central to the workings of the Navajo

economy, society, and culture. The Navajos obtained additional livestock through three main methods: purchase, trade, and what we might term long-term loan without permission. The Navajos wrapped livestock in their own stories and eventually emerged as the most powerful Indian nation in North America.[1]

When one thinks of Navajo identity, one thinks not only of sheep but also of weaving. The Navajos incorporated the wide vertical loom of the Spanish into their weaving. Early Navajo weaving was also influenced by Spanish design elements. Before the United States wrested authority over the Southwest from Mexico, the Navajos also began their association with silversmithing. The squash blossom necklace should have been called the pomegranate blossom necklace because silver beads in the necklace actually represented pomegranate blossoms. The horseshoe-shaped emblem at the bottom of the necklace could be traced to the Islamic symbol of the crescent.[2]

The Spanish colonial enterprise in the valley of the Rio Grande as well as sporadic outbreaks of smallpox prompted many Navajos to continue their general movement to the west. The Navajos gained greater command over the extraordinary country in and around Canyon de Chelly and Canyon del Muerto. Peach trees and cornfields numbered among their noteworthy farming achievements.[3]

In contrast to many Pueblo communities along the Rio Grande, the Navajos could not be corralled or controlled by the padres. The Navajos thus played a rather secondary role in the great revolt that swept through the Southwest in 1680. Fragments of Puebloan communities feared Spanish reprisal in the wake of the 1680 revolt. The Navajo clan system expanded to accommodate many of these newcomers. Many of these clans have continued into our own day, including, for example, the Coyote Pass clan, whose roots extend back to Jemez Pueblo. Other clans apparently may be linked to other groups of widely varying origins. The Naakaii Diné clan is a case in point; in the Navajo language, "Naakaii" meant "Mexican." The overall willingness of the Navajos to attract and to absorb different groups obviously contributed to the expansion of the Navajo presence and ultimately to Navajo ascendancy prior to the arrival of the Americans in the 1840s.[4]

The second era comprised the years the Navajos called "the Fearing Time." It began with the assumption of authority over the Southwest by the United States following the conclusion of the war against Mexico in the late 1840s. It ended with the signing of a major treaty between the United States and the Navajo Nation in 1868. Thus, within a generation, the United States moved with alacrity to impose that control. Americans believed they could make major changes in the character of the Navajos only by imposing an alternative environment upon them. The adults seemed incapable of fundamental change, but the children offered more hope. General James Carleton, the officer in charge of the New Mexico Territory's military presence, argued in favor of removing the Navajo children from their home country and placing them in boarding schools a long way from what he termed the "haunts, the hills and the hiding places of their country." In such institutions they could learn "the arts of peace" and "the truths of Christianity." Eventually, the "old Indians" would "die off and carry with them the latent longings for murder and robbing" and the "young ones" would "take their places without these longings and thus, little by little . . . become a happy and contented people."[5]

Carleton believed that unless the American military took charge of the situation through an active, ongoing program of forced removal, the Americans would realize little success. After observing the United States build a fort, with the symbolic name of Fort Defiance, and send soldiers into Navajo country with limited success, Carleton decided in 1864 upon a brief, blunt campaign spearheaded by none other than Christopher "Kit" Carson to force the Navajos to surrender and to make a long journey into exile. A miserable winter offered additional incentive for departure. However, the "Long Walk" exceeded even the worst fears of its participants. After deadly traumatic forced marches, those Navajos who survived found themselves at the hastily constructed Fort Sumner, hundreds of miles from their home country.

In the stories they told, the people remembered the Fearing Time. They recounted their wells being poisoned and their peach trees being leveled. They recalled the old ones and the pregnant women who could not keep up with the others on the forced march and who

were shot by American soldiers or left behind on the trail. They told of the people who had never learned to swim and who had drowned when they attempted to cross the Rio Grande. "We will never forget their screams," Luci Tapahonso later wrote, "and the last we saw of them—hands, a leg, strands of hair floating."[6]

Thousands of Navajos avoided the Long Walk. They fled to the north and the west to places such as Navajo Mountain and Black Mesa, where even today you can avoid capture if need be. Many of these individuals remained in these areas after 1868 and thus contributed to Navajo geographic as well as economic expansion. Fort Sumner awaited those who could not escape or who chose to remain with children or elderly family members. They now had to reside upon a different earth. They had to live under a different sky. And, of course, they could not know how long they would have to remain here, but there appeared to be no reason to believe they would ever be allowed to return home. Hunger, illness, and disease stalked this unfamiliar terrain. Only the ceremonial leaders seemed able to provide some small element of hope for today and tomorrow.[7]

However, thousands of miles away a change in American Indian policy enabled the Navajos and some other Indian nations to sign final treaties with the federal government. Given similar goals for different Native communities, these agreements would have a certain manufactured look about them, as they reiterated the importance of schooling or access to reservation land by railroads.

In May 1868, federal representatives William T. Sherman and Lewis Tappan arrived at Fort Sumner to negotiate with Barboncito and other Navajo representatives. Sherman initially encouraged the Navajos to consider Indian Territory as an alternative location for their home. Barboncito emphasized his belief that the people must reside within the boundaries of their sacred mountains. When Sherman and Tappan finally agreed to permit the Diné to go back to their home country, the Navajos were overjoyed. In what must be ranked as the two most famous sentences in Navajo history, Barboncito replied: "After we get back to our own country, it will brighten up again and the Navajos will be as happy as the land. Black clouds will rise and there will be plenty of rain."[8]

While other treaties—particularly the 1868 Treaty of Fort Laramie—would become notorious as an agreement that the federal

government would not live up to, the Navajos helped to fashion a document of enduring power. The day the treaty was ratified in time became a Navajo national holiday.

A gathering on the Northern Arizona University (NAU) campus in the summer of 1999 reaffirmed the day's value. During the past year, a copy of the treaty had been on display at the NAU library. Countless Navajos made long journeys just to see these pages and to pay their respects. Evangeline Parsons Yazzie commented, "I think the treaty was lonely. I think it missed us." Speaker of the Navajo Nation Edward T. Begay praised the leaders at Fort Sumner who had given "us a land, a home within the four sacred mountains, and a purpose as a people to live with our new partner, the United States, as a nation and as a semi-independent entity within these borders." By their stance in the negotiation process, he declared, Barboncito and his colleagues had made a lasting mark on Navajo history.[9]

The final period is the Americanization era from 1868 to the early 1920s. During this time the federal government pushed for the assimilation of Indian nations. One commissioner of Indian affairs even concluded with unconscious irony that it was certainly time for Indians to feel at home in America. The Americanization era featured a heavy-handed emphasis on "genuine patriotism," focusing on America as their true home rather than "some paltry reservation." Those Indian students who could be convinced to attend school at distant boarding schools far from their families were subsequently pushed to obtain employment in their new surroundings.

The late nineteenth and early twentieth centuries witnessed massive immigration to the United States by immigrants from around the world. Many of these newcomers came to the American West in search of new opportunities. This rapidly growing contingent sought land in the region; Indian reservation land bases quickly became targeted for use by these folks. Non-Indian farmers and ranchers already residing in the area joined in the clamor to subdivide the Native estate. The Indians had more land than they needed, and their emphasis on land being worked by extended families conflicted with an established preference for nuclear families.[10]

The General Allotment Act of 1887 devastated many Indian nations. Following the model of the Homestead Act, under the provisions of the Allotment Act each Indian adult male would be eligible

for a quarter section of land, with any remaining land conveniently eligible for subdivision and subsequent sale.

The quarter section of land provided for in the Homestead Act might have been well suited for a prospective farmer in Iowa. However, a prospective rancher from western North Dakota needed more land to have even a fighting chance for survival. Other headaches soon surfaced, including inheritance. If a family possessed 160 acres and the family had four children, the next generation might include each person holding 40 acres. Given such inadequate totals, leasing or sale emerged as handy options.

Over the course of several generations, then, the map of an allotted reservation began to resemble a crazy quilt. On a reservation such as Pine Ridge in western South Dakota, the Indians actually own or have control over less than half of the land. Pine Ridge is the home of Russell Means and other Lakotas unlikely to ever be awarded the Nobel Peace Prize. Other federal decisions, including the aptly named U.S. Supreme Court case of *Lone Wolf v. Hitchcock*, reiterated the power of Congress to modify any treaty with or without the consent of members of an American Indian nation.

For every three acres of land the Indians owned or controlled in the mid-1880s, two had vanished by the end of the Americanization era. At the same time, in stunning contrast to most other Indian nations, the Navajos increased their land holdings significantly. Executive orders combined to add land to the reservation in 1878, 1880, 1884, 1886, 1900, 1901, 1905, 1907, 1911, and 1917.

Although some allotment of Navajo land did take place in the so-called checkerboard area in the greater Crownpoint area, that process constituted a different situation because of the land grants bestowed to bolster the development of railroads. Otherwise, the main Navajo reservation essentially escaped land allotment. Why wasn't it allotted? The answer is more complicated than that Nazlini didn't look much like Nebraska.

A more complete response mirrors an ongoing pattern. The Navajos had to fight against the imposition of this practice. In 1914, Chee Dodge wrote to Secretary of the Interior Franklin Lane strongly rejecting the idea of inflicting allotment on the Navajos. He says in essence: "Don't do it. Don't even think about it." "The character of our reservation," he notes, "is such that its division or

allotment is not feasible and would prove our ruin . . . the reservation ought to be kept intact and land within the reservation ought to be secured for us." Here is an obvious example where leadership made a difference.[11]

Other foundations for the future emerge at this time. The question of Navajo land use had already become a controversial one. Federal agents rehearsed arguments that would be presented in the 1930s when the livestock reduction program was more fully imposed upon the Navajos. They have nothing good to say about what they deem "the worthless ponies" about whom the people appear to be, oddly enough, especially fond. On the other hand, they seem unwilling to acknowledge the fact that non-Indian ranchers are perhaps overgrazing their livestock even more than the Navajos may be.

During the first years of Peterson Zah's life, the Navajos struggled with issues related to authority and control. The late nineteenth and early twentieth centuries illustrated the problems inherent in a colonial relationship. For example, the person in charge of the Shiprock Agency, William Shelton, was determined to punish any and all Navajos who went against his will. Shelton started throwing so many Navajos into the Shiprock jail that the local Navajos began to call the jail "Shelton's hotel."[12]

Outside corporate interests profited from a relentless campaign that implied that all Navajos lived either in Monument Valley or in Canyon de Chelly, wore squash blossom necklaces twenty-four hours a day, and did not consider their day complete unless they went out of their way to drive their sheep through towering red sand dunes. Although the local white people generally appeared to have little good to say about them, the Navajos over time discovered the French and the Germans had little bad to say about them and seemed willing to make timely investments in the local economy.

The Navajo Treaty of 1868 included a requirement that Navajo children must go to school and that for every thirty children who could be "compelled" to enroll the government would be responsible for employing teachers. In this period, Navajo children began to have options in regard to what kind of school they would attend as well as its location, but even if the alternatives increased, most of the options remained inadequate. Many parents chose to keep their children out of school altogether.

The children who went off to boarding school not only were separated from their families but also were susceptible to serious illnesses and even death. Navajo parents frequently agonized over the kind of treatment their children received in the dormitories, and for their part, children who had reached their limit in punishments for a variety of transgressions might protest against such treatment by running away. The theme that resounds from this era is the lack of Navajo say in the overall process, and this in turn once again sets the stage for Peterson Zah's day.[13]

A final example from this period may be found in the origins of the Navajo Tribal Council. Individual entrepreneurs and various corporate enterprises attempted to gain access to Navajo mineral resources. The Bureau of Indian Affairs convened several regional councils, but the first truly reservation-wide entity did not meet until June 7, 1923, in Toadlena. Discussions in Toadlena and in subsequent sessions revealed some of the representatives beginning to look beyond parochial perspectives.

Would the Navajos matter in the generations to come? Would they be able to gain greater control over their lives and lands? By the time of Peterson Zah's birth, the Navajo Nation confronted crucial questions about what it stood for and what it could become. The Navajo Nation had no guarantees about its future. The people had learned, however, they must become directly involved in the overall process. The Navajo Nation faced a great many questions, most of them quite complicated and most of them not easily answered.

Four Corners Area

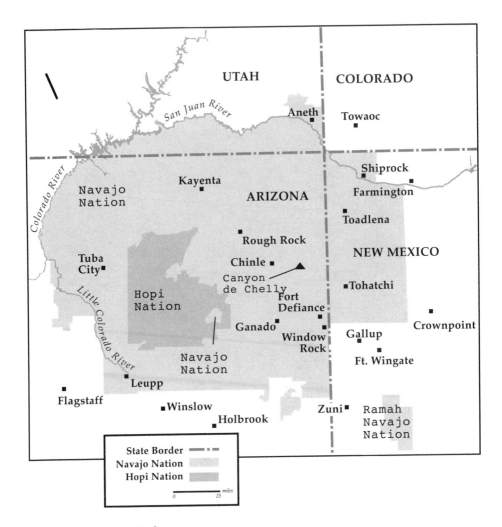

The Navajo Nation Today

1

Generations

"You Have to Share What You Have and You Have to Work Hard"

THE NAVAJO WORLD INTO WHICH PETERSON ZAH was born in December 1937 revealed both significant continuity and sweeping change. He grew up in what social scientists termed a traditional extended family. The Navajos had demonstrated through the centuries a capacity to incorporate new elements and over time make them their own. Livestock furnish an obvious example.

Long before 1937, the Navajos had developed a society in which members of multigenerational households could work together and through their livestock holdings know prosperity. Zah's grandparents contributed considerably to his upbringing. His family resided in the Low Mountain area, about fifteen miles from Keams Canyon, Arizona. His mother never attended school and never learned the English language. His father enrolled in school and remained there for eight years, thus receiving more education than most Navajo children of his era. He later served on the Navajo Tribal Council.

The Navajos believed that they should reside within the boundaries marked by four sacred mountains. They linked each of those mountains to a season, a direction, and a color. They proclaimed Mount Taylor in New Mexico to be the summer mountain, to be the mountain of the south, to be adorned with turquoise. In "This Is How They Were Placed for Us," poet Luci Tapahonso declared

the sacred mountains "were given to us to live by." She proclaimed: "These mountains and the land make us strong. From them, and because of them, we prosper. . . . This is where our prayers begin."[1]

The people shared a language and certain elements of a dynamic culture. In 1937, however, they had not yet become a single, unified political nation. The Navajo Tribal Council had been imposed on them in the early 1920s, but it could not yet be considered as incorporated. Most Navajos lived a long way from the newly constructed capital, Window Rock, Arizona. Grandparents, parents, and children formed units that could be economically, culturally, and socially viable. They credited their success to the goodness of Mother Earth and the generosity of the Great Spirit. Even when times proved difficult, even when there was little food to eat, the people generally assumed better days would come. They believed, as Tapahonso wrote in "A Birthday Poem": "Our lives were set by precise prayers and stories to ensure balance."[2]

In the twentieth century, however, the Navajo world became progressively less insular and more unstable. Outside interests clamored for access to Navajo mineral resources and grazing lands. Many non-Navajos complained about soil erosion on the reservation and realized that the old ways could not be entirely sustained if the people themselves could not take better care of the land.

Livestock reduction accelerated a movement already underway. Tribal Council delegate Ned Hatathli noted in 1957 that as early as 1931 only 50 percent of Navajo individual income had come from the raising of livestock. By 1956, that percentage had dwindled to less than 10 percent.[3] As early as 1947, Tribal Council delegate David Clah dismissed sheep as "a thing of the past."[4] To be sure, most Navajos did not share his point of view, but the fact that such a sentiment would be articulated at all attested to changing times.

The bitterness created by livestock reduction ultimately could be traced more to the cultural than to the economic significance of livestock. In October 1933, Tribal Council chairman Tom Dodge (the son of long-time leader Chee Dodge and the brother of emerging leader Annie Dodge Wauneka) addressed the council and provided a candid judgment on the condition of the Navajo range. "I know from my own observation that the reservation as a whole is very

much overgrazed," Dodge said. "We ourselves should take the lead in dealing with the question of erosion. We should not be driven to it by outside people. We should not hold back hoping that the conditions will better themselves without our help."[5]

As Dodge's speech made clear, the Navajos were not automatically opposed to developing an appropriate initiative. Unfortunately, Commissioner of Indian Affairs John Collier felt compelled to move at a far more rapid pace than the people wanted. Current market conditions made it almost impossible to find buyers for excess Navajo livestock, and thus many of the people's animals were simply seized, shot, and left to rot. If Collier had been willing to compromise on the pace and scope of stock reduction, leaders such as Tom Dodge might have been able to forge some kind of pragmatic arrangement. But that goal could not be realized.

At the very least, the Navajos argued, they should be treated as equals. Elsewhere, Tribal Council delegate Roger Davis pointed out, farmers were being paid for not producing more meat or more corn. However, Navajo farmers and ranchers did not receive similar support.[6] Other forms of inequality also surfaced. Navajos fought and died for America, but then came home and were denied the right to vote.

Even though Peterson Zah had appreciated the benefits that came through a family that embraced the values of mutual respect, sharing, and hard work, he also began to perceive the vulnerability of that social unit. That, in turn, encouraged his own reconsideration of his personal goals. Going to school would probably take him away from his family. However, as his father and some other family members began to suggest, perhaps schooling might offer him a way to gain the preparation necessary to defend and represent more fully and effectively his family, his community, and his people.

Traditional Teachings and Beliefs

Zah: The traditional Navajo people really believe that we individuals must respect the earth. You always have to be thankful for what the earth has to offer. And in our situation, living back in Low Mountain,

there was no difference between what the traditional Navajo people taught the young ones of each generation. The earth provider is food to ourselves, to our animals, and all the living things out there. You have to respect Mother Earth. That means that when it rains, particularly during the female rain season, you have to sit down, you have to pay attention to what the Great Spirit is trying to tell us. By these natural forces such as rain and snow, the Great Spirit is talking to us through some of those kinds of events and some of those movements that happen only by the force of the Great Spirit.

Early on you learn that. In my situation, that was something that I was taught by my grandparents. Respect for all other living things. It's something that one individual living out there has to really, really appreciate. And I guess because of those kinds of teaching, I carry that later on in life, where I respected everybody. I respected things, I respected the woman population, what they brought, and I guess because of those kinds of feelings, I worked very closely with Annie Wauneka, and I made her my adviser, because she was able to bring a different perspective into my administration. Something that you hardly ever hear other people say, she would be one of those individuals that gave that loving advice. I know that when she's talking to you, she has this motherly instinct when she talks to people. And you can't help but just listen to her. Maybe it's because of those early-on things that I learned that I was able to respect people like her.

It's something that I think every individual, whether they're Navajo or not, should have to practice—is the respect they have for the living things out there, including the earth. Because the earth is alive.

Everyone has certain beliefs. Mine was the Navajo traditional belief. People go to church; they have their own religious beliefs. I didn't really pay all that much attention to all of the other religions because I knew I was a Diné, and I was brought up to believe that there is a Great Spirit watching over each and every one of us. And that was the Navajo teaching that I got from my grandparents and from my parents. I have practiced these traditional Navajo beliefs throughout my life. I may not go to every ceremony and participate intimately during those ceremonies. But my beliefs were there. I could not go to every religious event that happened in my community and even with your friends and your relatives.

The San Francisco Peaks, the Navajos' sacred mountain of the West.

It's something that I think every Navajo individual needs to pay attention to, because nowadays there are many people out there who are trying to entice the young Navajo to go their way, and they're always trying to recruit them into their own religion. And we, as a Navajo people, have to weigh each one and try to say to ourselves, "Which one fits me, and which one is something that I will end up really, really believing in?" But you only decide that after you do your own research and after you ask a lot of questions. That's how you decide. The Navajo people are so fortunate in having those kinds of beliefs—where you believe in the living things, you believe in everything that's alive such as animals and the sky. The whole system of the universe that's out there, that only the Great Spirit can make.

When I'm passing one of the four holy mountains like the San Francisco Peaks near Flagstaff, or Mount Hesperus near Durango, Colorado, or Dibé Nitsaa, you stop for a minute and you give a blessing to living things out there, because what it does is that it brings to you a certain beauty that man cannot do. When I see the beauty of the San Francisco Peaks and the beauty of one of the four

holy mountains, I always think to myself, Now, we can't do that. We can't make something like that—we, as people. Man can't do it. Only the Great Spirit, and through the Great Spirit's mind and hands—the Great Spirit and the deities that lived back then were the only ones that can do that. They were empowered by God to do that. They got these things, and they left these things behind, so that we can see that and retain our aesthetic values—our sense of beauty.

In today's world, sometimes we live so fast and there are so many things that are happening—many, many negative things that are happening. You can't turn on a television each day and expect to hear some good news. And so when you come by either one of those four holy mountains, a beautiful lake—you have to stop and you have to pay attention. You have to pay respect to those places that the Great Spirit has put those things before man's eyes. And I always appreciated it that way. Not necessarily do the Navajo people pray to the mountain, but they pray through the mountain to get to the Great Spirit, and I think there's a distinction between the two.

My Parents

My father had about an eighth-grade education, and he was one of these individuals that sought education; he wanted to learn the white man's language, white man's culture, and the way the non-Indian people do business. Because of his desires, he was able to enroll and get some education.

My mother, on the other hand, never went to school. To this day she doesn't know how to speak English. They were very, very good partners in terms of raising children, because one was a very traditional person, and the other one had some education. They mixed the two very well. I'm the oldest of their eight children. We had instilled in us the values of Navajo tradition. We continued to talk Navajo and to live traditional Navajo. We didn't even know we were living on the Hopi reservation. There were all these meetings and negotiations taking place right about at that time between the Hopi Nation and the Navajo Nation and the federal government. The federal government partitioned the land and put a fence around the original Hopi reservation. We ended up on the inside. So we

were given notice, and we were told that we had to move out of there. Our family had to pick up the pieces and move outside of the Hopi reservation, towards Low Mountain. We were able to gather our things and start chopping some trees to make our home there.

Life in a Traditional Family

We always lived north of Keams Canyon. We lived in a valley that is north and east of Keams Canyon. I don't really remember how old I was, but that's when I really started noticing things. It was a family gathering place where my grandma and my grandpa lived, and we always lived right close to where they were living. Of course, they had some sheep and they had some horses, and maybe two or three cows that they owned. I remember going out with the older boys and tending to that. That really built into my head when—even when I was just a young man, a sense of responsibility. We all had to help to keep the family going, to keep the traditions going within the family. And we had to be able to take on some of those responsibilities that the elderly expected of us. So it is something that I always remember, and today I sometimes dream about living back then.

Navajo sheep mingle in the Tuba City area, blissfully unaware of the incipient federal livestock program.

We planted corn. We planted all of the basic food that we would need: squash, beans, potatoes—those kinds of basic staples—watermelons, pumpkins. We had to make sure that they were good crops to be picked in the fall. Our water supply, I would say, was maybe a couple miles up the canyon and into the mesa there. We had to dig up our own water. And we used an old shovel, any kind of steel that we could find, and we would dig into the earth. It looked like the water was seeping out, and then you'd make a little pothole into the clay. That's where the water accumulated every day and each night.

In the morning you'd come with a bucket, and you'd take that water home. During the night, it would accumulate, and some more water would come out, and the next morning you'd take another five-gallon bucket to get that water. And of course the sheep had a windmill closer to the highway—maybe about four or five miles, that's where we took the sheep. But drinking water was one of those commodities that was hard to come by. I think about that today. We drank all of that water, just coming out of the earth. How come we didn't really get sick? I guess your body just gets used to it, because all your life you've been drinking that water, you build up an immune system to any kind of a virus. It's just amazing, just to think about those things.

Back then—and I would say this was probably in the early 1940s—you didn't really hear all that much about the Navajo–Hopi land dispute. We were already living in Land Management District 6, which is the Hopi territory. It wasn't until perhaps during the war in the mid-1940s that I heard a lot about those kinds of local discussions—local politics, and where the Hopi Nation was really trying to push out the Navajos who were occupying some of the spaces within Hopi territory.

We had to move on several occasions from Keams Canyon, going up farther to the east and the north side of Keams Canyon. Every time we moved, we would move maybe eight miles up or ten miles up, where we settled. The settlement was such where you had to dismantle your hogan, and then we had an old wagon—a John Deere wagon that my grandfather owned—and we would use that wagon to haul all of the logs that we used for corrals, and for the hogan. It was hard work, but it was also good for our bodies and good for our minds and our souls because we were actually doing things.

Toy Stories

Back in those days we didn't really have what you call toys. Nowadays, I live with my grandchildren, and everything they have we buy for them—the parents buy it for them. They just end up accepting the toys as they are, as they are made, coming out of the factory. And there's nothing that goes into thinking about how those toys are made.

But when we were that age, when we would have some time to ourselves, we would go over to the mesa where there was a lot of moisture, and we would dig into the ground and dig out the clay—the clay that the Indian people used to make pottery. And we would get that and we would create our own toys. If we wanted to have a horse, we had to draw our own horse, we had to shape the clay into a horse or a cow or even little things that we would need. So I guess when at such a young age, when you do those kinds of things, a lot of your own creativity is instilled into you. And you then become a creator of your own toys, and you have to do things in such a way that you make things for yourself. You make your own toys, and you have to find places, and a time when you can be alone and play. And play the things that you like to play.

So I think people of my generation, they learned how to do all of that, for which I am very grateful. We didn't buy things from the store. We had to create it and do all of those things and find it ourselves.

There's a lot of talk about people having to move from the Navajo–Hopi land-dispute area. And the way Navajos talk about it, and it's very, very emotional for the Navajo people. But the way I look at it is that we already had to move three times. My family had to move outside of District 6. And then when we did that, we didn't move far enough, so we ended up into a disputed area where the land was jointly owned by the Hopi and Navajo.

When that got settled in 1974, we had to move again outside of that area because where we were living became Hopi country. The mediator and the federal government made it so that they turned that land over to the Hopi Nation, so we had to move out of that area again. It just gave us a lot of strength. It gave us some of those things that pulled the family together. My grandfather always said,

A Navajo family shears a sheep. Sheep figured prominently in not only the Navajo economy but also the workings of Navajo culture.

yes, we are having a tough time, we were having to work hard, we don't have much to eat and all of that, and every day we have to work to build our own dwelling place, our hogan. And we had to rebuild the corrals and all of that. But you know, this is going to make us a stronger family. And for you young boys, it's going to make you stronger individuals, where you have to do things on your own. You don't depend on anybody. We're not dependent on anybody; we're having to do all this ourselves, and so I'm teaching you a lot about self-reliance. And sure, there are going to be challenges in life. This is just a good lesson for you to go through.

That was something that I experienced during my lifetime. My grandmother and grandfather were very strong people traditionally. My grandmother never went to school and didn't know a word of English. My grandfather had some schooling. He went to a vocational school and learned carpentry. He knew how to do a lot of these things. He spoke perfect English. He also spoke the Hopi language and spoke the Apache language. So he was in every sense

of the word, trilingual. He was a very resourceful person. He was the person that held the family together.

A lot of my uncles and some of my other relatives served during the war. That left us at home, the young boys, only with the women. Because of the war, my uncles and my father and other people had to leave the camp.

Hunger

We were so hungry. We didn't have much to eat. What we ate was what we found out there. We were so hungry that we started talking about killing our own horse—the little pony that we had in the family that was really cherished by many of the youngsters within our family. That was really a terrible emotional experience that I went through because we were taking care of that little pony, and we had to slaughter the pony in order for us to survive. When we got together, we'd talk about how you kill an animal. Well, with a sheep it's very easy, you just get a knife and cut their throat. But how do you kill a horse? After some discussion, the ladies in my family decided that my mother should be the person responsible for killing the pony. She told us to put a cloth over the pony's eyes and hang the cloth on the ears, on the two ears, so that the pony can't see. And then she got an axe and hit the pony in the forehead, and the pony went down. That was our food for the next several days.

So we had to do those kinds of things in order for us to survive. I guess in my case, you have to learn from that. Anything you do in terms of raising your own food, you always have to save. You always have to save some of the vegetables that you may raise during the summer, that you harvest in the fall, for the winter. And you have to dig into the ground—into the earth—where you refrigerated the food. That was in many ways our refrigerator. So in the winter we would go to where our food was stored. It was one of those situations where when you're eating something, you also have your little small siblings, brother and sister that were smaller than you. You always have to keep them in mind because they want to eat too. You don't want to be so picky, so you eat just enough to have the food go around so that you survive another day.

During the 1930s, most Navajo girls learned to weave, usually being taught by an older woman relative. Certain design ideas and patterns in Navajo weaving could be passed down from one generation to the next among family members.

That was a great lesson to all of us. I vividly remember many of those experiences. I learned that you have to share whatever you have, and you also have to work hard even to get your own food to eat for the day. It was a good lesson for me and for many of us to go through that experience.

In the Low Mountain area, some families had a house and transportation. They had pickup trucks or highways, trading posts, and electricity lines to take care of their basic needs. We never had those. When we moved from place to place, we had to go down into another valley. There were no roads. So how do you get from the top of the mesa to go down into the lower section of that land? We had to build our own roads. And build them so that even the horses could be driven down the valley. In many cases we had to work not for one week or one month; we had to work years just to do our own roads so a wagon could go down. And so that was the kind of environment that I was raised in.

My grandfather was the one that really promoted that. He organized the community, and we all came out and had fun together, but at the same time we were working hard—working really, really hard with the shovel, with the sledgehammer, with all of the basic manual labor–type tools. Crowbars and all of that—we used to build our own roads.

Responsibilities

I was a young man, but I was expected to take on a lot of responsibilities because I was the oldest child. I had to help dismantle the hogan and the corral and herd the sheep over to a new place, which became our new home. The war had broken out, and my dad was called on to go into the services. Ultimately, he became a trained Navajo Code Talker, but the war ended before he was able to use those skills he had learned.

There were only a few schools on the Navajo Nation at the time, and they were mainly elementary schools operated by the Bureau of Indian Affairs because they had what they called outside-the-reservation boarding schools for children who were in the ninth grade

Navajo children learned about responsibility by looking after the family's sheep.

on up, or eighth grade on up. These were just small, small community schools. Keams Canyon was one of the very few schools for young children, and it was always occupied with schoolkids. There was hardly any room for everyone's children to enroll there. The school was too small for the community. So I ended up being left out. That's why I didn't go to the Keams Canyon Boarding School.

My grandma and my grandpa always lived with the family in the same community. There were a lot of discussions about my future and the future of other children. They really weren't so sure if it was the appropriate thing to do to get an education. Some members of my family wanted to have me become a medicine man. I showed, at a young age, some interest in what the elderly people, particularly the medicine people, had to say. And I exhibited that by going and joining them at the sweat bath, or at a local ceremony. When the medicine men would come in and they would do their ceremonies and they would bring their paraphernalia, I was interested in that, and then I was interested in their prayers and their songs. And my grandfather and my grandmother kept on saying that I was very interested in seeing and listening and looking and talking with some elderly folks.

I guess for me, it was really about gaining knowledge. I was motivated to learn from the elderly and what they had to say or sing or the prayers that they used. And they looked at me as a kid being interested in all of that.

2

Schools

"I Needed to Get an Education"

DURING THE 1930S AND 1940S, NAVAJO family members faced difficult questions about whether their children should attend or continue to attend school. The federal livestock reduction program had forced Navajos to wonder about the viability of their traditional economy. If fewer children would be needed to help with the sheep, then more might be able to go to school. Tribal Council delegate Sam Gorman recalled that when "the opportunity presented itself for me to go to school, I ran away all the time and finally it became permanent." "My education might have been a bright light for my people," he added, "but today I do not possess that." Those who lacked education, he concluded, were like a bird with only one wing trying to fly.[1]

World War II also prompted reassessment. The Navajo Code Talkers became the most highly publicized Navajo contributors to the war effort, but they were hardly alone. Other Navajos joined other military units and worked in war-related jobs, including the Navajo Ordnance Depot in Bellemont, Arizona, and the Fort Wingate Ordnance Depot near Gallup, New Mexico. Experiences during the war gave Navajos a new sense of the contemporary American economy and the kind of preparation they might need in order to participate more fully in its workings.

Through their time at school, Navajo boys and girls learned a variety of lessons. Students and parents did not always have the same reasons for children attending school nor did they necessarily use the

same criteria for evaluating the significance of this experience. More than a few students reiterated that while they missed their families when they were away at school they persisted because they wanted to have more options in the future. Some boys were drawn by athletics and the chance to compete against other teams from other Indian schools or from non-Indian institutions. Most successful students did not spend a lot of time agonizing over how ideal the schools should be. Zah later remembered he "didn't suffer as long—as much as the other children did." He had concluded that in order to "begin to be self-sufficient as an individual" you had to go to school and that in all likelihood that school would be away from home. That was just the way it was: "It was something that I had to deal with in my life."

Many non-Indian Americans expressed surprise that Navajos and other indigenous communities would, in fact, turn out to enlist in such impressive numbers. But those who enlisted often spoke as much to a commitment to one's own Indian nation as to loyalty to America. One of the original Navajo Code Talkers, the artist Carl Gorman, designed a special patch for the Code Talkers' uniforms. The illustration revealed a parallel between what the Code Talkers were trying to achieve and the goals of the legendary figures from Navajo cultural history, the Hero Twins, who fought to rid the Navajo country from monsters who threatened the people. Now it had become the task of the Navajo soldiers to rid their two nations— Navajo and the United States—from contemporary monsters who threatened their future.

A Navajo Tribal Council resolution passed at the end of the war noted that of the twenty thousand children who could be enrolled in school, only six thousand actually attended. Many of the existing boarding schools were overcrowded, and the day schools continually confronted bad roads, insufficient vehicles, and other shortcomings. Peterson Zah assumed he would attend school in relatively nearby Keams Canyon, but the overcrowded school had no room for him when he finally decided to go there. Instead, he joined cousins at the Tuba City Boarding School—a site so removed from Low Mountain that he did not see his parents at all during his first year.

Soon after the war's conclusion, the Navajo Tribal Council presented requests to the federal government for assistance in getting

the Navajos ready for this transition. "Education is our greatest need," council members proclaimed. "Our people are now very poor. Our children must have a good education if they are to learn to support themselves." And "without education we cannot compete with the white man anywhere."[2]

Two very different perspectives permeated the world of American Indian education. Both reflected regional and national trends. During the New Deal years, the Bureau of Indian Affairs attempted to move away from the heavy-handed assimilation of the past several decades. The bureau hired linguists to develop more effective orthographies, so that Indian children would have a better chance to learn to both read and write in their native language. For Navajo students, writer Ann Nolan Clark composed the *Little Herder* books. These volumes provided stories about young children and the world in which they lived. Graced by Navajo artist Hoke Denetsosie's illustrations and an accompanying Navajo-language text, these bilingual, bicultural texts were way ahead of their time.[3]

Yet in 1946, the Republicans began to gain more power in Washington, and the bureau pendulum started to move again toward assimilation. Although more Navajo students gained access to high school, they encountered a limited number of options at the secondary level, almost always centered in vocational-technical training. Zah got caught in this clash. He enrolled in Phoenix Indian School, and as he neared the end of high school, he thought about going on to college. However, his teachers generally refused to write in support of his application. "You're a fine carpenter," they told him. "You aren't prepared for college."

Peterson Zah would eventually make his way into and through Arizona State University (ASU). This journey made evident the results he could achieve, regardless of how many discouraging and disparaging perspectives he might encounter along the way. "You had to be pretty determined," he recalled.

This is vintage Zah. "OK," he is saying, "so you don't think I can do it? Just watch me." It also is obvious the difference a key individual could make as he or she made his or her way into unchartered terrain. In the ensuing pages we are introduced to Joe Famulatte, a football and basketball coach at Phoenix Indian School who went out of his way to encourage Zah to continue with his studies. We are

also introduced to Bob Roessel, who helped develop the program in Indian education at ASU and who subsequently played a central role in the establishment and development of the Rough Rock Demonstration School and Navajo Community College (now Diné College). These and others reminded Zah about the difference an individual could make. It would be a lesson he would always remember.

Going to School

Zah: I kept on saying that I needed to get an education, that I needed to learn how to speak the white man's language, and to learn more about the way they do things, their lifestyle, and some of the things that they valued. It was not necessarily to become one of them, but to learn about them. And to become aware of and knowledgeable about all of the other things that the white man was able to bring to the Navajo reservation, including, for example, cars, the buildings, the language, and the writing skills. My dad thought that I should learn all of that. And that it will make me a better person.

The community of Keams Canyon was about fifteen miles from the Zah residence in the Low Mountain area.

Playground at Keams Canyon Boarding School. Peterson Zah had assumed he would attend the boarding school closest to his home, but Keams Canyon Boarding School was already full by the time he tried to enroll.

A tremendous pressure was laid right on my shoulders, where I had to make a personal decision about enrolling in school. My aunt Julia had several boys, big healthy boys—my first cousins. One day they came to our hogan, and they said that they decided to all go to school at the Tuba City Boarding School. They said we had to drive all day to get there because there were no highways. It was gravel road and we had to go through the Hopi Nation, and that we would be going through many of the Hopi villages. So one day, they said that you need to get ready, we'll come on this day, and we'll take you. I was so happy I cried.

My only question was what do I need to take? They said the only thing you need to take is some clothes that you own, and that you should just jump in the pickup truck with us, and we'll go. But I didn't have any clothes. The only clothes that I owned were what were on my back. And then they said that, well, we'll give you some clothes—you're still a small boy, and your bigger cousin has out-grown some of his clothes, and we'll give those to you. So I was all excited. It was a big decision. It was sad, because I had by that time

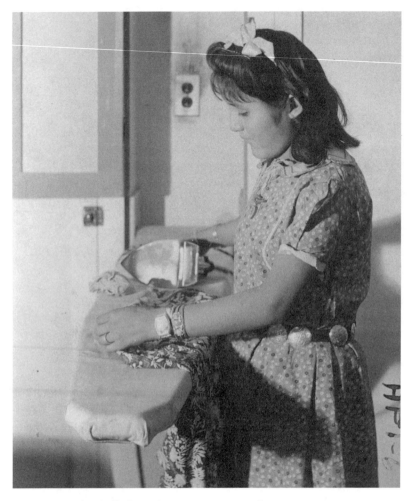

A Navajo girl enrolled in a home economics class at Keams Canyon
Boarding School irons a dress.

three or four small sisters. And it was one of those days where on
the one hand you're happy that you're jumping in with your cousins
to go to school; on the other hand, you're leaving your mother and
father behind, and at such a young age—I was about nine years old.
But there just weren't any schools close by our community.

I remember we had to stop twice to eat. There were maybe
only one or two gas stations. And finally we ended up at Tuba City

Boarding School in late afternoon. When we got there, I thought it was strange to see all of these big, huge buildings, made out of beautiful sandstone. And that kind of caught my eyes and my curiosity, because there were so many rooms, and it had two, three floors. The dormitory aide said that this was going to be your place to live. And they had two dormitories, one for the big boys and one for the small boys. They took me to the small boys' dormitory. And I remember when I checked in, they gave us a small bag, full of tooth powder, brushes, soap, and some towels and they said this is going to be your bag. And all the things that you need are in here.

They gave us two real nice white sheets for our bed. They said one is for to cover your bed, and the other one is to cover you. You had to sleep in between. They were cold. Then they also gave us some extra blankets and towels. Then they said there are going to be about thirty-five, forty other students in this room, and they put our names on the beds. I didn't have any underwear. I just had two pairs of pants and maybe two shirts, and maybe a jacket to keep me warm. That was about it. My shoes were either too small or too big for me, and I didn't have socks.

The cafeteria was located between the two dormitories. And when I first went to eat at the cafeteria, there was a large variety of food that you could have. There was some meat; there were a lot of vegetables—corn, watermelon, squash, spinach, beans, tomatoes. I could identify some of those because we tried to raise some of those back home like potatoes and beans. But I didn't know how the others were raised or where the school got them.

So that was kind of like my curiosity, and it got me asking the kitchen workers where they got the vegetables. Those questions led me to a place called the Pasture Canyon owned by the school where they raised all these vegetables. I was interested in the agriculture program and spent many weekends working on the farm. I signed up. I ended up going to the pasture canyon many weekends, learning how to plant food and vegetables, and learning how to take care of horses that they used to plow.

Iverson: Do you think that having family members—relatives going to school at the school when you got there—did that help you in terms of sort of adjusting to that different environment?

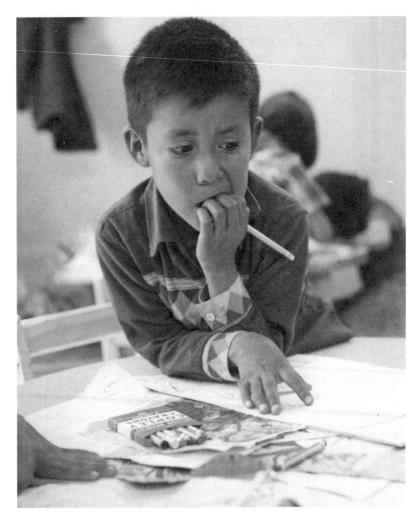

A young Navajo boy takes on a new environment.

Zah: The adjustment was very hard for me personally. It was hard because I loved my mother and my father and my grandparents. The idea of leaving them and the animals behind—your horses and sheep. That was very emotional for me.

Iverson: I would think so.

Zah: But I also knew that it had to be done that way. We would just have to make that break and begin being self-sufficient as an

individual. One concept was that you had to go away from home to get an education. So that was something that was very strong in my own mind, and that's why I didn't suffer as long—as much as the other children did. As long as I accepted that concept in all the other things, it didn't matter that much. It was something that I had to deal with in my life.

Iverson: Were you able to see your mother or other persons at all when you first started in the fall until later on? Did they ever come over to see you, or was that discouraged?

Zah: My aunt Julia, whose children were going to school there, we saw her maybe two, three times a year. I think maybe on one occasion my mother would come with her.

A Typical Day

Iverson: Please describe a typical day at the school, how it started, and what you did.

Zah: The boarding school was conducted almost like your military institute where they separated the boys between what they call the big boys' dormitory and the little boys' dormitory. But within that dormitory living, they had what they called a platoon system, where you were each given a number. And you all had to get in line first thing in the morning—let's say seven o'clock in the morning—and you had to stand on your number when the whistle blew. Prior to that, you had to wash up—you had to brush your teeth, you had to comb your hair—you had to make up your bed, and you had to have nice, clean clothes on. And you had to shine your shoes.

The food included a lot of vegetables, milk, juice, and toast. The dormitory aide was there to make sure you ate your food. So we had a lot of cornbread. We had a lot of beans. We had watermelon, we had corn, and all of that.

A typical day for me was going to my English class to learn more about how to communicate and what the words meant. Then the next hour was devoted to learning more in working with your hands in the wood shop class. We learned something about tools, and learned something you could make with your hands.

Farming played a vital role in the lives of most Navajo families during the time of Peterson Zah's childhood. This cornfield was situated in Canyon de Chelly.

It was a vocational education class and then the next one might be physical education, where we played baseball, football, basketball, and those kinds of activities, just to exercise your body. But they really didn't have any showers. You did that just in your plain clothes—the clothes that you were wearing. You didn't go to a gymnasium. There was no gymnasium at the school.

At noon we went back to the cafeteria for lunch. The cafeteria was set up in such a way that you were each given a duty. Some of the students had to cook, and so they were given permission to leave at eleven thirty or quarter after eleven, for example. They worked at the kitchen until all the students started showing up at twelve. And they served us food, and then afterwards they would stay until about one thirty.

Then in the afternoons, we would go back to class, maybe to take a math course. Learning how to add, learning how to subtract, learning how to divide, learning how to work with numbers, and all

of that. And then maybe in another class, we would learn more about hygiene—something about the study of our own bodies, minds, and spirits. So there were a lot of health-related discussions.

Iverson: And was almost all of that instruction in English?

Zah: All of that instruction was in English. And for those students that needed some interpretation, you had to ask for a special bilingual instructor to help you with the teaching. But none of the students really prided themselves on going to that person, because they didn't want the other students to know they weren't getting what they were being taught in English. It was kind of an embarrassment. You just had to blend in with the rest of the other students when we were being taught English.

Iverson: You read about and you hear about people saying that at one point they tried to discourage, one way or another, students from speaking Navajo, or whatever the case might be, in the dorms. They wanted you to speak English. Was that the way it was there?

Zah: At Tuba City Boarding School, it was a situation where the staff and the teachers discouraged that. We were too young to feel the brunt of that policy, where they would get a little stricter. Because we were just too young to really have the staff try to enforce the concept of not speaking Navajo. In my situation, I didn't really know that many English words. So the challenge was just to learn more English words.

Staying Away

It was very rare for parents to come visit us. I remember, even at some points I got so lonely. I got so lonely for my parents that you'd hide behind a tree, and privately cry. But at the same time, you didn't want to have the other boys see you cry, because that was looked upon as not being manly, and perhaps still being a little boy. Boarding school life was hard, but we didn't have a choice.

Once you got dropped off at a boarding school, we never got back in contact with our parents. My father had obligations with the United States Marine Corps, and he was in and out of the service at the time. And so the month of May came, and we were told that we're

all going to take you home. I remember getting in the back of the truck, and we were driven all the way back to Keams Canyon. When we got to Keams Canyon, they'd call out your name—who gets off at Keams Canyon Trading Post? And I remember I was one of the people whose name was called. I didn't have a suitcase or luggage or anything like that—it was just a paper sack with all my belongings.

My mother was sitting over on the north side of the trading post underneath a tree waiting for me. And when I went to her, I remember, she broke down crying and said she had missed me. I was wondering how come she was crying. She said, "I'm just happy—happy for you, that you have grown, you're a big boy now, and you look a little different." So it was a happy cry on her part.

She then said, "We have a wagon here, and we want you to drive back." She was with my grandfather and one of my sisters. We drove back to where we were living, some twelve, fifteen miles away to Low Mountain. That was my first year in school, and it was very intriguing—a lot of learning for the first year.

In the next year, I went to what they call the big boys' dormitory with my cousins. I remember when I went to that second dormitory at Tuba City the thing that really caught my eye was a man by the name of Byron Tsingine. He was a tall Navajo person, nice-looking, and he had two or three little boys. He was just such a wonderful, wonderful man and educator. Byron Tsingine was the one that taught me a lot of things about growing up and in the future what I should be. He was very, very concerned with every kid that was going to school there and always talked to them in Navajo.

Now, at the boarding school in Tuba City, the teachers and the boys' adviser all wanted us to use the English language. So they really frowned on speaking the Navajo language unless it was necessary like talking with our parents.

The Importance of Sports

I got interested in and involved with athletics at Tuba City Boarding School. We had a baseball team, we had a basketball team, and we tried to have a football team. And so there was a lot of physical activity that took place. However, there were no organized sports

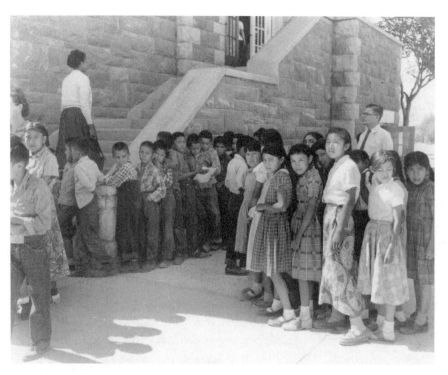

These students attended the boarding school in Tuba City, where
Peterson Zah began his schooling. This photograph was taken in 1956, a
decade after Zah was enrolled here.

between schools at the time. We simply played against each other or
between dormitories.

My cousins, when they outgrew their clothes, would always give
them to me. That's how I was able to generate enough clothing so that
I could remain in school. I had to learn to shift for myself at an early
age, and my desire for a decent education was never compromised.

From the Tuba City Boarding School, I went to a Flagstaff public
school called South Beaver because my father got a job at Bellemont,
west of Flagstaff. That was during the Korean War. A lot of the
Indian people were called in to the services to help the United States
and the armed forces to load ammunition and put it on trains. They
were sending those across the sea for our armed forces to use in the
war. He worked there for several years, and I went to South Beaver
Elementary.

Phoenix Indian School

Then I signed up to go to Phoenix Indian School. We were always poor. This time I had an old suitcase and gunnysack to carry my clothes. I saw where all the boys had these nice suitcases, and they used to laugh about how I was carrying my clothes. So that was probably my biggest moment getting on that bus and being driven, along with probably thirty or forty students, in two buses that came all the way across the Navajo Nation into Holbrook, Winslow, or Flagstaff, and then Phoenix. Seeing these palm trees, and all of these cities—like the big, tall buildings—that was really something to see. I was excited to see all these new things I had never seen before.

When I got to Phoenix Indian School, I was enrolled in what they called the Special Navajo Program. That was a five-year program; it was not a regular high school. It was a special program initiated by the federal government for those students who were late in enrolling. We were too old or big to start class at elementary level, and that's why this program for Navajo students was initiated. You could only go to school there for five years and receive a certificate in vocational education, plus they got you a job. The challenge was to accelerate your learning experience and skip two or three grades in one year and then go into the regular high school program. Instead of bad-mouthing the system, I decided to go at my own speed and pick up some grade and enrolled ultimately in the regular high school program.

The high school across the street had athletic teams. They had football, basketball, track, and baseball. And we went to their games, and I really became interested. I wanted to play, but the school policy did not allow students from the special program to be on the high school team.

I then asked my teacher what it would take to transfer to the high school. She said work and study hard and do well on your tests and maybe skip a grade and next year put you in the regular ninth-grade class. I spent the year working hard in high school and the following year became eligible for all the other school activities. And I joined a team in basketball, football, and track my first year there, as a tenth grader. Boy was I happy, thinking this will keep me

sane at this terrible boarding school. Subsequently, I was elected as treasurer of the student council and in my senior year served as vice president. That's how I got interested in school government, and we began talking school issues and policies. My interest in student government then led me to bigger issues in tribal and state as well as federal government.

Sports occupied my mind and time. Because going to a boarding school was difficult. You're isolated, you live in a dormitory, you live in a compound. You don't really have access to the outside world. And participating in sports and all of these school activities keeps you occupied and does not allow you to go crazy. It was kind of like my way out of the boarding school system.

Vocational Emphasis

They didn't have the best academic situation there. The teachers taught a lot of vocational education. They looked at their job as educating the Indian students, having them become painters, electricians, carpenters, and sheet metal workers. Then if you graduate, they'll find you a job and turn you loose in the private world. The school wasn't really geared towards college, because there were only a few students that went on to college and university. When I was graduating in 1958, it was really scary, thinking about how I had been in the boarding school system all these years, where I got my food, I got my bed, I could stay there and keep on going to school. And I never really had to worry about myself and how I would function in the outside world. Approaching graduation during my senior year, I kept wondering about these things. The school is going to kick us out of this campus and then what do we do next. It was really a very scary feeling.

I then decided that I should go to college. But to enroll at a nearby community college, I had to have recommendations from my teachers as part of the admissions process. None of the teachers that I had would recommend me as an academic student capable of doing college work. I remember one teacher telling me that "I don't want to embarrass the school and myself by saying that you're college

material and that you should go on to college, because you're just not. You're a carpenter and good laborer. And that's as far as you probably will go—you should remain there. Don't agonize about the idea of improving your stature by thinking that you're going to make it in college. So don't bother me." And so that kind of angered me—I was mad. I thought to myself, well, that teacher doesn't know me that well.

The only person that probably knew me well on that campus was the basketball coach Joe Famulatte. I went to the coach, and I explained my situation and my desire to go to a community college somewhere within the state. I told him I was having a tough time trying to get at least three recommendations from teachers. The coach then said, "Or you could go to Phoenix College, which is just down the street. And you could walk there and you don't need transportation." The coach was really responsible for getting me started at Phoenix College.

And when I enrolled, I met the basketball coach, and he put me on the team. And for that, I got tuition waived and I was able to negotiate a good price for my meal ticket and purchase books. Phoenix College treated all of us good as long as we were on the team. Coach Famulatte offered his home, where I stayed during my freshman year and worked on his rental homes on weekends. It was really nice of him. I graduated from Phoenix College in 1960 with an AA degree. Then I went to Arizona State University in Tempe, a huge university, I thought at the time.

Iverson: Earlier, you said when you decided to go to college that teachers at Phoenix Indian School didn't necessarily think that was a great idea.

Zah: Most of these boarding schools—like Phoenix, Fort Wingate, Albuquerque, Intermountain, Sherman Institute, Chilocco, Oklahoma—were not really geared towards putting the students into colleges and universities. They were just not equipped to do that. We were seen as incapable of doing any college-related work and more suited for working with our hands and putting us into the community workforce. But there were a few students from all of these boarding schools that went on to college. They were exceptional students that beat the odds and became highly motivated.

You Had to Be Determined

You had to be determined and find your own scholarship, to find your own way to a university. No one really helped you. There were no college scholarships, for example, offered by the Navajo Nation. They didn't have a scholarship program. And so when I came here and went to Phoenix College and ASU, there were no Navajo scholarship programs.

Iverson: And there weren't many Navajo students.

Zah: Yes, exactly. That's why we only had about a dozen Indian students at ASU when I got here, seven or eight Navajo students here on campus.

Phoenix College

Iverson: Tell me a little about what it was like going to Phoenix College. As I recall, some of those buildings had just been constructed through the WPA funds and other federally funded programs. That was a bit of a bridge for you. It was a transition that helped you get ready for ASU in some ways.

Zah: I decided to go to Phoenix College because one, it was closer to Phoenix Indian School. And number two, a coach, a basketball coach at Phoenix Indian School by the name of Joe Famulatte, a famous Indian school coach, really encouraged me to go to Phoenix College. He had some conversation with the basketball coach there, and so one day Coach Famulatte called me into his office, and he says, "If you want to go to Phoenix College, you can get on the coach's program and play some basketball there."

Iverson: Where did you live?

Zah: I lived for a while at Phoenix Indian School during the first semester. But then I had to move out—I believe it was in December or January. Because there were more students that were coming in at Phoenix Indian School, and I had to leave and give my room to those incoming students. And so Coach Famulatte just picked me up and he says that "you can live with us, we just have one spare room, and you can live there and you can walk to Phoenix College."

I walked every morning from 3rd Street on Indian School Road all the way to 14th Avenue on Thomas Road. Every morning. And once I had made the basketball team, then I got to know other players on the team. Then they gave me a ride back to the dorm—back to the Phoenix Indian School campus, at the dormitory. And so I was able to make those kinds of arrangements by getting to know some of those players.

Iverson: Were there other Indian players on the team?

Zah: There was one other American Indian student on the team, and that's Rodney Lewis. Rodney Lewis went to North High School, and he was one of the better players in the city of Phoenix back then. And he did very, very well.

Iverson: He is from the well-known family at Gila River.

Zah: Yes. He is from Gila River, a member of the tribe. And his father was a minister at the Presbyterian Church at 3rd Street and Indian School Road. And many of the Indian School kids went to his church. Just a really good, solid family. And one that really believed in education. So Rodney Lewis had a good background, because his family was so strong in community affairs—worked with many, many of the Indian people here in the city of Phoenix.

Iverson: Tell me more about playing basketball at Phoenix College.

Zah: I made the team, but unfortunately during the season, I really got beaten up. My tooth was knocked out. It was broken in half, and I had to go to the Phoenix Indian Hospital to take care of it. And then the other thing was that my ankle—I had a broken ankle right at the lower half of my ankle in high school. That never really healed. It was always with me. The doctor was advising me that when you break an ankle like that and you stay in bed, and you stay in bed for so long, you get tired of staying in bed, and then sometimes you think you've got well, so you start using your feet again—you start walking again.

Iverson: Maybe too soon.

Zah: And yes, the first day it won't hurt, but what you're really doing is that you're using it before it gets completely healed. If you keep on using it and keeping on using it, it never really heals up. You're just damaging your ankle. Well, when I was at Phoenix College, I sprained my ankle in the same side, in the same place. And that was really painful. It was the most painful thing that I ever

experienced. At nights it would swell up. And the doctor said that "you're just going through a painful process towards healing your ankle." The only thing that they could do was just give me some strong medicine to take care of the pain.

And they didn't actually treat it. And yes, I did have a brace that they put on, but then you got tired of that, too. So you ended up taking it off because you couldn't wear shoes. So you got tired of that too. That's what happened to me during my first year at Phoenix College. I ended up dropping basketball halfway through the season because of the pain and the need to have two good legs to walk to school.

Arizona State University

Iverson: Tell me a little more about deciding to attend ASU. Did you think at all about going somewhere else to school?

Zah: I didn't really think about going anywhere else. I enrolled at Phoenix College in 1958, and I went to school there for two years. And then in 1960 I came to ASU. I really did not think about going anywhere else except to go to ASU.

That was because I knew people here in the city of Phoenix, people that I could rely on for help. And I couldn't rely on my parents, because they weren't working. They were living 330 miles away from Phoenix, on the Navajo Nation. You had to learn how to shift for yourself.

I didn't have a scholarship, but I went to ASU and I told them I could work in exchange for their assistance. All I wanted was to take some courses and try to extend my education that I had started at Phoenix College—I wanted to add onto it and get my degree in education and go back to the Navajo Nation as a teacher. That was my goal. It was something that I really, really focused on, that was what I wanted from ASU. ASU responded, and they put me to work.

When I graduated from ASU I decided to have a small party. I invited my former teachers at the Phoenix Indian School who had refused to recommend me for college. I sent out all the invitations, but I didn't hear from any one of them. The only person who was happy

for me was the coach. He said, "I knew you were capable and you just became a role model." He said, "Congratulations," and he even wrote me a little note.

The point is that there were few opportunities for Indian students to attend college at that time. The teachers kept saying, "We're a good school, we're a vocational school. We're not trying to prepare students for college. We believe that most Indian students are better off going into the community with some trade that they learn here. And they're very good with their hands, and they're good workers." That was the reason they gave me for not recommending me.

But in every group of students, some have higher goals and aspirations. I guess I was one of those individuals. All I wanted was a simple recommendation that said that I was capable, could apply myself. That's all I wanted, was that opportunity. The door could become open and get me into a small community college which really wasn't very different from an Indian school. That's all I was seeking. But unfortunately, they didn't agree with that goal.

Iverson: In addition to Coach Famulatte and Bob Roessel, was there anyone else affiliated with ASU who also played a key role in your studies at ASU?

Zah: The other person that people never really ever heard about, but in my own mind he was also very helpful, was a professor named Dennis Keegan. He kind of took an individual interest in me, because I was different in his class. I was completely different than the other students. He saw my work, what I was capable of doing, and the work that I was performing in his class was also a little different than the rest of the other students. He encouraged me to keep working hard. He also made arrangements for me to do my student teaching at Tempe High School during my final semester. He taught cabinet making, welding, wood finishing and designing, and student shop maintenance. He was just a great teacher and he loved what he was doing. We all admired him for that.

Iverson: What kind of work was that?

Zah: He was an industrial arts teacher where, for example, one of the courses that he was teaching was what they call finishing, where you work with metal and you do finish work, fine work. Where you weld things together and make sure that it holds and it's strong, and then you sand it off with a sander, and then you finish all of that and

make sure whatever it is that you put on is also something that stays on. And he taught the same thing with wood—the different kinds of wood, and how you finish, and what materials you use to finish wood. And some of it had to go into cabinetmaking, and designing different things, and how the factory designed different things that we use in our homes.

He also taught finishing work on cars, vehicles, how you can redo the body of a car, and then how you can paint it and what you have to use. A lot of handwork. And I guess Professor Keegan saw that I liked doing that kind of work, and so he kind of gave me some extra work that I could do to improve my grades, for example. He's still around—he comes around every once in awhile.

I went to Arizona State University for three years, and I graduated in 1963 with a degree in secondary education. I went to work at Window Rock High School. Going back to the Navajo Nation and working with my own people was an ideal job for me. I always liked working with the young people.

It was at this time in my life I married Rosalind Begay, whom I met at ASU. She was an education major. We had a lot in common and shared those interests together. I eventually met her brother, Harvey Begay, an ASU alum, who became a lieutenant and a pilot in the Navy and flew phantom jet fighter planes during the Vietnam War. Rosalind became a great advisor, supporter, and mother of three children—Elaine, Eileen, and Kééyonnie—and now ten beautiful grandchildren.

Then while teaching at Window Rock High School, I got a little disgruntled because I thought I was limited and confined to a classroom. I was also interested in what was on the outside—looking out the window—and I wanted to do more with the people out there. One day, I was talking with some friends that were working for the tribal government, and they said they had a position open at design and construction. They were looking for construction estimators, someone who could read a blueprint and figure out how much the building was going to cost, materials for the building, and labor cost. I applied and got the job and started working with more people in the construction industry.

As a construction estimator, I was able to read blueprints and figure out the labor costs and the material costs and then about

how long it will take to build those facilities. That was challenging. You had to really, really study the blueprint. You had to understand the work of the architect, and then you had to understand your labor force and all of that. I really liked it, and I liked working there for about two years. And then one day, Bob Roessel, the late Bob Roessel, gave me a call. And he says, "There's a guy that you should meet who has a grant from the federal government. It's a program that is like the Peace Corps program. I want you to meet Mayland Parker. He wants to talk with you, and you will do a good job for him in training the VISTA volunteers and getting involved with some of that volunteer work."

VISTA Training

I came down from the Navajo Nation to talk to Mayland Parker, who explained to me that ASU had received a federal grant to do VISTA volunteer training. The VISTA volunteer program was a spin-off of the Peace Corps. It was something that ASU was very proud to receive. VISTA volunteers were volunteers that came to ASU for their training, and those students were then assigned to an Indian reservation. And not necessarily with any specific duties, except to help the community. They were supposed to write proposals, make contacts for the local communities to outside businesses, and write letters, write resolutions, and in many cases get involved in school, community activities, and all of that. But before they went out, these VISTA volunteers had to be trained and become sensitive to Indian cultures and become more appreciative of Indian wishes.

So during the training program, while they were on campus here at ASU, we worked with them and placed them, during the training, as part of the training process and put them out in Indian communities. And my job was to bring them together in the evenings and have lectures on what they experienced during the day. And they were trying to get themselves involved and off the ground with some of the projects that they were involved in with local communities.

My job was to help the volunteers. And it was done right here at ASU. I did that for two years and I really enjoyed working with

many, many American Indian leaders, who were not only from here in the Southwest but also from other parts of Indian country. I took these volunteers to visit local tribal governments. I also went and drove across the country to places like North and South Dakota, and in Minnesota and Oklahoma. My job was to visit people out in the field and give them some encouragement and then try to correct some of those things that they ran into as volunteers.

I cherished the friendships that developed while we worked together. Volunteers didn't have friends to use to start projects or give to local communities. They were paid a stipend for their work. They had to be able to start projects and organize a community around an issue locals wanted solved. VISTAs were mainly college-educated people that volunteered their services for two years.

3

Leaders

"You Have to Have a Vision"

IN MANY INDIAN COMMUNITIES, leadership is something that runs in the family. If your father held this position or your aunt had taken on that responsibility then you may be more likely to be called upon to take on a particular task. And sometimes from an early age you may begin to ponder the prospect of leadership.

One can certainly see in this chapter that leadership is a subject of considerable interest to Peterson Zah. The very fact that he wanted to place this section at this point in the book reveals its importance to him. His father's participation on the Navajo Tribal Council no doubt encouraged that concern.

Throughout modern Navajo history we can see examples of this involvement. The most prominent instance is the Dodge family. Henry Chee Dodge and his son, Thomas Dodge, both served as chairman of the Navajo Tribal Council, with Tom Dodge also becoming the first member of the Navajo Nation to receive a law degree. Chee Dodge's daughter, Annie Dodge Wauneka, became the second woman ever elected to the council and represented the Klagetoh area as a council delegate for several decades. She gained national recognition for her work in the area of health care, but an examination of Navajo Tribal Council minutes makes evident her extensive engagement in a wide range of issues confronting the people.

Zah singles out three major Navajo leaders for extended discussion: Manuelito, Annie Wauneka, and Raymond Nakai. Manuelito, a

Henry Chee Dodge, the grand old man of Navajo life and Navajo politics, played a central role during the first half of the twentieth century in regard to Navajo land holdings. Dodge helped expand the land base and worked with Anselm Weber and other allies to defeat attempts to reduce the acreage of the Navajo Nation.

famous resistance leader during the Fearing Time, believed strongly that Navajo children needed to get the best education they could in order for them to represent the people as fully and effectively as possible. So he sent his sons and his nephew all the way to Pennsylvania to attend the Carlisle Indian Industrial School, founded by Army officer Richard Henry Pratt. But, tragically, the three boys died from tuberculosis. Navajo historian Jennifer Nez Denetdale is a direct descendant of Manuelito's wife, Juanita, and in her recent book, *Reclaiming Diné History: The Legacies of Navajo Chief Manuelito and Juanita*, she interviewed Peterson Zah about Manuelito's response to this tragedy. Zah told her that "Manuelito was a man of great vision who knew the consequences of white society for the Navajos and had foreseen the benefits of Western education, not for turning Navajos into whites, but as a tool to better our society."[1]

The Navajo connection to Carlisle has been exaggerated because of Manuelito's prominence and the well-known before and after photographs taken at the school of Navajo student Tom Torlino. However, given the distance of Carlisle from Navajo country as well as its image as a school with a harsh environment, it is not surprising that few Navajo students attended the school before it closed during World War I and that no Navajo ever graduated from it. Available evidence indicates Torlino survived and returned home and became a farmer. A small number of Navajo students also attended more-distant schools, including Jacob Morgan, a future chairman of the Navajo Tribal Council, who went to Hampton Institute in Virginia.

Zah calls Wauneka the person who "probably did the most of any Navajo leader," because she anticipated difficulties "and then she did something about them." He refers to her as "a great leader, teacher, and role model." Zah observes that both Wauneka and Navajo Tribal Chairman Raymond Nakai employed the radio to furnish information and news to the Navajo people. Wauneka hosted a program on a Gallup radio station (Pet Milk sponsored the program, and as a result, Wauneka became known to many Navajos as "the Pet Milk lady"), while Nakai broadcast the news in Navajo every morning on station KCLS in Flagstaff.

In his broadcasts, Nakai often made remarks critical of the current Navajo government. Most Navajos relied on the radio to learn about what was going on in Navajo country, and over time Nakai became

very well known. He eventually served two terms as chairman of the Navajo Tribal Council. Nakai was the first modern chairman, noteworthy for his eloquence in both English and Navajo and for his general commitment to Navajo empowerment. He also supported freedom of religion in the Navajo Nation and as chairman made an important contribution to that goal by greatly reducing persecution of the Native American Church.

Navajo leadership could be observed outside of as well as within the council chambers. For example, two Fort Wingate High School graduates, William Morgan and Kenneth Begay, made major contributions to their fields of interest. Morgan became a pioneering student of the Navajo language. Working with linguist Robert Young, he helped develop an appropriate and useful form of written Navajo. Morgan also showed great patience and a well-developed sense of humor in teaching Navajo-language classes. Kenneth Begay learned silversmithing at Fort Wingate. He became one of the leading Navajo silversmiths of his day. His work demonstrated again and again his creativity and his capacity for innovation. As did Morgan, Kenneth Begay taught at Navajo Community College during its first years.

The ongoing opportunities and complications inherent in modern Navajo life could inspire a person like Ned Hatathli to take on a variety of responsibilities, from head of the Navajo Arts and Crafts Enterprise to Tribal Council delegate to president of Navajo Community College. In whatever capacity, Hatathli reminded people about obligations of one generation to prepare for and encourage the next. Zah and Hatathli voiced important themes. They believed a leader had to anticipate difficulties and to come up with creative solutions. Both recognized the fundamental difficulties facing the Navajo Nation, including an economy that struggled to absorb a growing labor force. "It has been mentioned here in the council time and time again," Hatathli said in 1955, "that we want to keep this Navajo Nation as a Nation." But in order to achieve that goal, he argued, the Navajos had to develop economies that would offer good jobs to younger members of the Navajo Nation. "Otherwise," he concluded, "they will go elsewhere."[2]

Political leader Peter MacDonald did go elsewhere. He attended Bacone College in Oklahoma and then transferred to the University of Oklahoma, where he received a degree in engineering. Then he

worked as an engineer for Hughes Aircraft in southern California before returning to the Navajo Nation to be in charge of the Office of Navajo Economic Opportunity (ONEO).

As Zah notes at the conclusion of this chapter, many of the ONEO programs proved popular, and in turn, MacDonald's own political fortunes soared. Although the two men eventually became political rivals, Zah does not hesitate to acknowledge MacDonald's successes during this stage of his career. He was, Zah believes, "an able, capable person" who at this point in his career "was looking out for the interests of the Navajo people."

Leadership Qualities

Zah: My own perspective on the issue of leadership is that every generation has its own leaders. They do whatever it is that they think should be done. And while doing that throughout history, they did a wonderful thing for the Navajo people. These qualities or attributes of leaders really come with time, because we have our own leadership qualities, abilities, and what we have to offer.

In terms of the qualities, I would say for Navajo leaders, one of those important attributes is the individual has to know the Navajo culture. They have to know the Navajo clan system—how people are all related to each other. There are things that come with those relationships. Every Navajo family has, for example, in-laws. They are married into another family. You know the clan system very well, then there are things like the teaching of Navajo individuals that comes into use by a Navajo who is very well versed in clan relations. The relationship between community members and their families— the knowledge on the Navajo culture, the knowledge on clan relationships, for me, was extremely important.

Individual leaders have to have a dream or vision. You can't just look at yourself as the administrator of the largest Indian tribe in the United States. You have to have a vision. How do you organize so that you get the Navajo Nation to get to be at a certain point in the history of the tribe?

One has to have an ability, skill, and knowledge not only in the Navajo language but also the ability to speak English very well, and

The federal officials had little good to say about the Navajo horses, but Navajo leaders resisted the drastic cuts in this part of the livestock economy. Here, a report on the program is being presented to the people at a community gathering.

then be able to articulate those dreams and long-term vision. For me, this was very important. I think that sometimes a quality that a lot of people overlook is the ability to simply articulate and connect with local people. But you can get lost in explaining what those visions are. And so an articulation of those dreams—your vision—I think is very important.

A leader has to anticipate what's around the corner on the other side, without actually looking at it. He has to be able to see the situation as it really is. An anticipation of what may be coming, I think, is also very important. You must be prepared for anything that may come your way.

I believe leaders have to experience traditional ways such as herding sheep, tending to the horses, planting their own corn, raising their own food. They have to have lived in a traditional hogan, and know the Navajo prayers. All of those kinds of traditional experiences bring behavior patterns that we need. You have to really be able to

understand those. And you can only learn these by experience. You can't really appreciate and learn those in schools.

You can only learn from your parents and grandparents and people in the community—all those kinds of valuable attributes. And you have to be able to measure your own ability against some of your own, for example, uncles and aunts and grandpas that live in those communities. So it's important that a person who wants to be a leader go through that process. It's something that I thought was important in much of what people did during the 1950s and '60s and '70s.

Hardship as Prologue

A person also has to have some kind of an experience where they go through hardship themselves. They must know how to react to those trying times. You don't really know the quality of a leader until those leaders take on a controversy or an emergency. See how that individual behaves and how well they handle the situation. And if there's some kind of a tragedy—or an event that really affects so many people—then you really find who the leaders are. Because you can't just go in front of the people and say, "I'm going to be your next leader." They have to see your heart, mind, and soul.

I admire the leadership of Navajo people in the past. If you look at the time when the Navajo people were imprisoned in Fort Sumner, at Hweeldi, you'll find resilience, the power of being resourceful and tremendous will to survive. We endured this hardship and these terrible conditions. There were many Navajo people who were imprisoned there by the United States government for four years. The Navajo leaders that were there, they were actually medicine men. Chief Manuelito is a good example. Ganado Mucho is another one. Some of the other well-known Navajo leaders were also imprisoned there. They survived because they knew the Navajo religion and culture. They knew the Navajo ways of life. They knew that you had to depend on yourself to become self-sufficient. The United States government officials thought that they might all die there. But our people survived. So they must have had something to survive these horrible ordeals.

When they were in the process of being released from Fort Sumner, the leaders did not fight over petty things. The important thing was to get back to their land; they wanted to get back to their loved ones that were left behind. They were homesick for their relatives and for their homeland. So they didn't fight over a little small detail while they were signing the treaty. They just said look, this gives us an opportunity to get back to our original homeland. And so they did.

When they got back it was just a small piece of elongated land that went from somewhere south of Window Rock, Arizona, going all the way up north along the state line and into Shiprock, New Mexico. They didn't fight over the small piece of land to which they were being asked to go back to.

Joined by others who had evaded capture and captivity, they all went to work to expand their land base. Each one of these chiefs, leaders, they all went back to work, and started adding to their reservation. Every so often—maybe every ten years—they would keep on adding to the Navajo Nation. So from 1868, millions of acres of land have been added. How did that happen? Why did it happen? I always say it happened because of Navajo leadership.

For that long period of time, over a hundred years, each one of those generations of Navajo leaders had the same goal. From 1868 to today, Navajo population has increased to about 350,000. The median age of the Navajo population is about nineteen years. We are a young nation for Navajo people. Therefore, the land has to grow as the population of the Navajo people is also growing. And none of those leaders ever said, "We shouldn't be doing that. We should be happy with the amount of acres that we have." They all did exactly the same thing from one generation to the other, which was to add more land to the Navajo Nation.

A Vision for the Long Term

I like the leadership of Chief Manuelito, because he knew what was happening and had a vision of the long term. He was the one that said, "What we now need is education." He said this at a time when the idea of sending Navajo youngsters to school was a bad thing to say to the Navajo people; he chose the route of increasing education

among our Navajo youngsters and to start sending them to colleges and universities. He said we had to learn how to speak English. We have to learn the white man's ways. If we can send our children to school, have them learn the white man's ways, then we can use education to fight them in their own way. Use the education as a way to win our battles. And so he didn't shy away from a controversy where the majority of the Navajo people at the time did not want to send their children to school. He knew what was necessary and good for the Navajo people.

He made sure that the Navajo families gave up their children to go to school. Because he knew it had to be done, because we were adding land to the Navajo Nation that would provide opportunities. He said let them become doctors, engineers, nurses, and leaders, and some day lawyers. And if we can do that, we can fight our battles.

Annie Wauneka is shown with her colleagues on the Navajo Tribal Council. Wauneka, from the Klagetoh–Wide Ruins area, Arizona, was the second woman to be elected to the Navajo Tribal Council. Elected in the spring of 1951, she would serve on the council for thirty years. Lilly Neil from Huerfano, New Mexico, was reelected in 1951 after serving her first term on the council; however, a serious auto accident two weeks after the election in 1951 forced her to resign.

Annie Wauneka was, I think, an individual that probably did the most of any Navajo leader. She did it because that was her personality. She did it without much education. She didn't have the greatest education in the world that one could receive; she didn't have a college degree. But she had qualities that most people admire. And those qualities were the ability to communicate very well with the Navajo people, in the Navajo language, on health issues, for example. She was one of these individuals who had the ability to see what's around the corner—that most people didn't see.

She knew what was coming. And so she anticipated some of these things and then she did something about them. When the Navajo people were being affected by tuberculosis—the Navajo people were dying left and right from tuberculosis—she did something about it. She single-handedly built all of those sanatoriums here in the Southwest. She went before the U.S. Congress to have them appropriate money so that Navajo people could have access to sanatoriums where they could be rehabilitated and get well. She visited them four times a year. She was a great leader, teacher, and role model for women and frankly all of us. She always will remain as one of my favorite Navajo leaders.

Leadership and DNA People's Legal Services

Iverson: When you were the head guy at DNA People's Legal Services that was obviously a leadership position. Tell me something more about how leadership was important within that. Was Ted Mitchell, the initial head of Navajo Legal Services, a leader, or was he just somebody that made everybody else unhappy?

Zah: I came to the DNA program as a young person. I had been out of college for only a few years when I was called upon to help lead one of the largest American Indian legal services programs in the United States. You have to look at that situation closely, where perhaps I was the only non-lawyer American Indian director at the time. That raised a lot of questions among lawyers, and from the county and state bar associations.

Ted Mitchell certainly was a leader in his own right. He received his law degree from Harvard Law School. He was one of those

individuals who was not afraid to say what was on his mind. He was an individual who was fully committed to his clients and cared a lot about the Indian people and the Navajo people. Everything he did was geared towards protecting the rights of individuals. Each person had certain rights. Mitchell was there to protect those rights and advised people that they should understand their situation fully.

Challenges Facing Navajo Leaders

Iverson: When you think about leaders in the past and the present—when you think about all of those challenges and difficulties that a president and chair would have to face—it's like they were joking on election night in 2008 about Barack Obama. They said, "If he wins, he should demand a recount." Because nobody should really want to take all that on. I mean, when you think about being elected president of the Navajo Nation, it can be a rewarding assignment, but it's also even more challenging, even more difficult, even more contrary than probably a winning candidate realizes.

Zah: I think the Navajo people have to recognize that being the Navajo president or chairman is not easy. Particularly if you look at the population of the Navajo, you have many non-English-speaking, traditional people that still hang onto the land. They still live the traditional lifestyle. You also have young people on that reservation that have master's degrees, doctoral degrees. And they're highly educated, and their demands from the tribal government or from the Navajo Nation are a lot different than the traditional people. Because of vast differences in between those two lifestyles—it just makes your job a lot harder. They each present different issues that are important to them.

And it takes a skillful person to deal with all of those complicated issues. If you were to look at the state of Arizona or the state of New Mexico or California, yes, they have their problems but their problems are similar—I don't think it's as hard as the Navajo. They can use television and radio to communicate with their constituents. The education and sophistication level of the local people makes all the difference in politics. You can reasonably expect that whatever it

is that you're doing, they'll catch on. They'll know and appreciate what you're trying to do. On the Navajo, you have that wide spectrum of beliefs and lifestyles, and that makes it harder. And so it's something that I think the Navajo people have to really recognize, in terms of the people that they elect to run their government.

Homeland

Iverson: The Navajos have been very successful in adding to their original land base and forging a kind of culture that is not a museum piece, but it's composed of many values and ideas. And despite all the difficulty, there seems to be optimism about the future. They have denied the image of the Vanishing Race that photographer Edward Curtis often attempted to impose.

Zah: The original reservation was small that the federal government designated to the Navajo people. This was located right in the Four Corners area, split in between New Mexico and Arizona now.

Regardless of how small it was, at least it was land that they could call their own. Undoubtedly, there must have been some Navajo leaders that said we should fight for more land. However, it was not the appropriate time to raise these issues. They just wanted to get home. Because they knew that when they go back, they have their whole lifetime in front of them, where they can demand more things, and increase their land base. And they all agreed that they would always continue to get more acreage and increase their land base. And for me, in looking back at the history of those traditional Navajo leaders, they had such great foresight. They had the vision that this was what they wanted to ultimately achieve as a group.

They also knew that they couldn't achieve that at the signing of the treaty in 1868. There was going to be resistance. They were very smart in doing what they did. When they said OK, we will grudgingly agree with the small acreage but that it shouldn't be the reason why we do not go back to our original land.

We want to go back to our homeland. We're lonely, we're starving here, and if we hold out, there may be more of us that may die. And so while we can, why don't we all agree that we will go back. And so as a result they signed the treaty and they went back.

Then the federal government told the people, "We're going to give each head of the family a goat and a sheep. And this is going to be your livelihood—this is going to be your food and survival."

Even then, they really took that to heart. Because they knew that they were getting something that would enable them to survive for years to come, and they would never have to starve. But they also knew that they could increase those numbers, if they managed that right, and it will take care of themselves, their family for generations to come. It would be their livelihood.

They didn't squabble over this by saying, "Hey, we want one hundred, or we want fifty," because they knew what they had in mind. It was a very smart move on the part of the traditional leadership in such a critical time. And so as a result, eventually, they were too successful because years later, the federal government came back and said, "Hey, you need to reduce your livestock. There are just too many animals around here."

Iverson: And why did the federal government say that at that time?

Zah: I think the federal government was looking at not only what they thought the Navajo people were doing in damaging the land, but you can always use something like that to get the sympathy of the decision-makers and some of the people that have to make decisions about the future of the Navajo people, or the land status that the Navajos were holding. There was some other underlying objectives, underlying desires. And that was to try to starve out the Navajo people even more. And that is something that the government said, "Well, they were damaging the land so we had to reduce our livestock."

Rationalization

Iverson: It's sort of a rationalization?

Zah: It was just a rationalization that they used to justify what they were doing. So basically, there were other things that one could assess and say, "This is the real reason." And I always think about mineral resources that were under the land that was given to the Navajo people.

The federal government perhaps realized at that point that it made a mistake in putting the Navajo people back onto the land that had oil, coal, natural gas, uranium, and timber. We had high-grade coal, one of the best high-grade coal deposits in the United States.

And oil was discovered on Navajo land. So when the federal government saw all these natural resources where they had put the Navajo, immediately they wanted to reduce or take back the land that was given to the Navajo. They also wanted to continue to deal with Navajo people in such a way that they would hold them down from the realization that they have all these mineral resources on their land.

But the Navajos didn't give in all that easily. They said that "you put us back on that land. You thought it was the most undesirable land out in the desert, no resources, no water, no grass, and all of that. And we accepted that. And now, after discovering all of these mineral resources underneath the land, then you want it back."

So they were very smart to do that.

Iverson: They were also being pushed by the livestock interest off-reservation in New Mexico and Arizona?

Zah: Sure.

Iverson: Because they wanted access to that land for their purposes?

Zah: I think the ranchers surrounding the Navajo Nation, outside of the Navajo Nation, many of those cattle growers and owners—people who make their livelihood on raising sheep and all of that—they wanted more land in addition to what they already had. And so there was probably a conflict between the Navajo people and the people from the outside. They started looking at Navajo land as land they could get back to developing into land for their cattle and livestock.

So going back all the way to the increase in land base, Navajo wanted to do that because they knew that the Navajo population was going to increase, probably at a faster rate than the nation's rate. They knew that, and that's why they wanted to increase the land base. Today we have over seventeen million acres of land in Utah, New Mexico, and Arizona. They wanted to also increase the land because of the natural resources and the natural beauty.

Annie Wauneka and Raymond Nakai

Zah: In the history of the Navajo people, there were two people that used the radio very effectively to set out their program—to advance their ideas for the good of the people. Dr. Annie Wauneka was one of them. Annie Wauneka was a woman that was ahead of her time. She was the first Navajo woman to serve many years on the council. Her father, Chee Dodge, was a tribal chairman. One of the things that she was interested in was the health of the Navajo people. And back in those days when I listened to her talk, the people would all say, "I want to be on the Budget and Finance Committee. I want to be on the Natural Resources Committee. I want to be on this and that committee." No one wanted to sit on the Health and the Alcoholism Committee of the council. But Annie Wauneka looked at that as a challenge.

She said, "Since nobody wants to chair the Health and Alcoholism Committee, I'll volunteer. It's a difficult one, probably one of the most important, but I'm going to take it such a way that I do it with a lot of pride. Not because I'm a woman, but because I believe I can do just as good a job as anybody else." And she never really used being a woman to her advantage. I think she looked at herself as a delegate that was able and capable, that was smart enough to establish a good viable program to improve the health of the Navajo people.

Iverson: She was in it for the long haul. She was determined to make a difference, not just from month to month, but from year to year.

Zah: She wanted to make a difference and knew that her time was limited when you go into tribal politics. So she wanted to do the best that she can possibly do.

She was one of these individuals that decided that from her position as a chairman of the Health and Alcoholism Committee, that she should take on the task of trying to eradicate tuberculosis on the Navajo Nation. At that time, many Navajos were dying and suffering from the contagious disease of tuberculosis. Navajo people really didn't know what kind of diseases they had, and the Indian Health Service was not really equipped to deal with these diseases in the most effective way.

So Annie Wauneka had to singlehandedly come up with some program or ideas to prevent more Navajos from getting the diseases. The use of radio was something that she came up with, where she went to a radio station in Gallup, New Mexico, and other places surrounding the Navajo Nation, and she had those radio stations give her some time to address the Navajo people almost every day. And then she had the Tribal Council also help the Navajo people with the purchase of some of those radios that they could have at home in their community.

Annie Wauneka talked about people's health and how to avoid the disease and spreading to other people or family members. She also addressed the U.S. Congress, because there were so many Navajo people that had contracted tuberculosis, they needed to be in a sanatorium. But they didn't have any such facility.

She went before a United States congressional committee and urged the committee to appropriate funds to build a sanatorium here in Phoenix, Colorado Springs, and Albuquerque, where many of the Navajo people came to cure their illness. You had three facilities where the Navajos went for rehabilitation.

She frequently visited the Navajos in the sanatoriums. She became an emissary between the Indian Health Service and the Navajo Nation.

Iverson: Sort of a cultural broker.

Zah: Yes. And that was her job, and as we all know now, because of her effort, she got the Presidential Medal of Freedom that was given to her by President Johnson in 1963.

She's one of these individuals that really took an effective use of radio to send her message out to the Navajo people to improve their health. That was her whole purpose. And it takes an extraordinary person to do that.

She was an extraordinary person, one of my heroes. I really admire all of the things Annie Wauneka was able to do for her people.

Iverson: I thought it was interesting how she formed this alliance with Scott Preston. Preston was a politically active religious leader who knew Navajos were going to have to take advantage of some elements of the Western healthcare system. Because he said, "Our ceremonies are important and they do a lot of good, but they don't—we don't have anything specifically that works fully against

tuberculosis, and we've got to find a way to meet these newcomer doctors and nurses partway, so that it can work."

Zah: The older Navajo leaders, such as Scott Preston, they were all traditional people. And they didn't really have a good command of the English language. But they were good, dedicated leaders. Fully dedicated to the Navajo cause, and that was the kind of people those individuals were. When they did their work and when they convened a meeting, the last thing on their mind was how much money they would get for their efforts.

And the tribal leaders weren't being compensated at such a high rate back then. So it was all based on pure dedication and the willingness to serve people. Just wanting to help, and being dedicated to the Navajo people. That was the tool that they possessed to get to where they wanted to go. And so they were motivated by the poor condition of the Navajo people and how they wanted to change that. Annie Wauneka represented that element of the Navajo politics back then.

The other person that really used the Navajo radio very well was Raymond Nakai. Raymond Nakai was working at Bellemont, west of Flagstaff, during the Korean War. He was working at what they call the Indian camp, where a lot of the Navajo people lived during the Korean War to do compacting and the assemblage of bombs and sending them overseas. They put it on a train, and then it got shipped across the ocean to Korea. A lot of Navajo people worked there. Raymond Nakai was one of those individuals that was in the community with the other Navajo people.

He was employed by the radio station, KCLS, in Flagstaff. And every morning he was on the air. And yes, he told news, he told current events in the Navajo language across the reservation. But in the end, something like the last five minutes, he would really talk to the Navajo people about what is going on with their tribal government that they may not know about. He got famous for the critical comments he made about Navajo government.

He was a radio person who broadcast news early in the morning. The Navajo people woke up listening to him early in the morning. When it was time for a tribal election, he put his name on the ballot and kept on campaigning using the radio, and that's how he won the election. He was identified as a Navajo person that informed them

Raymond Nakai became well known through his work on a Flagstaff radio station. This photograph was taken at his inauguration as chairman of the Navajo Tribal Council.

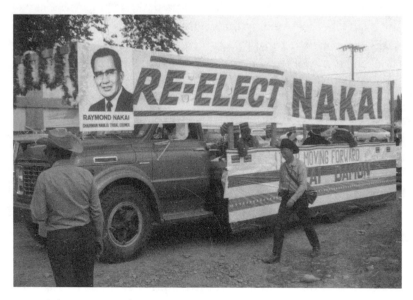

Part of the campaign for Raymond Nakai, seeking re-election as chairman of the Navajo Tribal Council.

each morning about some of the things that they didn't know was going on with their tribal government.

He played a vital role in the campaign to permit members of the Native American Church to hold their ceremonies without being harassed. He was the person who calmed everything down. Raymond Nakai said to the people, "Look, we live in America—in America, and through the constitution, we have freedom of religion."

Iverson: I believe that Raymond Nakai was a very important leader. He was noteworthy for his use of the radio, his ability to speak eloquently in both languages, and his determination for the Navajo to really be in charge of their own government and to reduce the kind of power that Norman Littell, the attorney, had held. I think historians and others have really not given him sufficient credit. He was a more significant figure than many younger people assume today.

Raymond Nakai became chairman when he was a relatively young man. He served for those two terms, and then Peter MacDonald came in after that. Mr. Nakai lived a long time, but it was difficult for him to find a proper role in contemporary Navajo political life.

Zah: Yes, I would agree that Raymond Nakai was one of those individuals that was very much dedicated to helping the Native American Church—helping the Church itself grow, where it would be respected by the tribal government. He tried to keep the tribal government out of the Church's affairs and to educate the Navajo public about what freedom of religion is all about and what it means.

He had a giant role. He was one of these individuals who used the radio very effectively. He was an excellent speaker of the Navajo language. He created Navajo words to explain what he was talking about. So he was in so many respects artistic in that fashion. Where he came out with words that nobody had ever used—never thought of using. But Navajo people caught on.

For example, people back then didn't know how to say or how to illustrate sovereignty. What is the meaning of Indian sovereignty? And he came out with this word using the analogy of the rainbow. A rainbow. And he said, "Sovereignty is like a rainbow, and we were created within that rainbow, and the rainbow is something that the Indian people believe in that comes from the Great Spirit. It was not something that was given to us by the coming of the white man or

any group of people. It was always here, and we were born into it." That's the way he explained the rainbow, and it was very powerful. And that was the creation on the part of Raymond Nakai to explain sovereignty to the Navajo people.

It's the same thing that Annie Wauneka did when using the Navajo language over the radio about tuberculosis. You did not see tuberculosis, and you did not really feel the effects of the disease at the time that it's affecting your body. Annie Wauneka came out with those Navajo words which said it's a disease that could eat into your heart. Your heart is going to diminish in size, and it won't function as well. So she came out with those kinds of words to make Navajo people understand. Raymond Nakai was the same way.

I always looked at my job that way. Never did I think that this was going to get me to the tribal chairmanship. You just had to keep on working every day and not think of those other possibilities in the future. They would become a distraction in your work. But what happened in the process was that there were some good cases that came to DNA. They raised issues that touched the lives of so many people.

And when you do that, you are protecting the sovereignty of not only the Navajo Nation but all Indian tribes. The name recognition is important in politics, and these kinds of impact cases gave me a high visibility in the community.

I became involved in other major court cases, including protecting sacred sites, water rights, and environmental cases. When tribal election time came around in 1982, there were a lot of pressures exerted on me to consider running for the Navajo chairman. I did declare my candidacy and won, and took office as chairman of the largest Indian tribe in America in January 1983. You don't plan those outcomes, they just happen with the blessing of the Great Spirit.

4

Lawyers

"The Navajo People Wanted
Solutions"

ATTORNEYS AND LEGAL SERVICES have had a great effect on the evo-
lution of the Navajo Nation and the lives of individual Navajos. In
regard to the Navajo government, the acquisition of legal counsel
helped transform this legislative body. There can be no question
that the expansion of what the Tribal Council took on was clearly
influenced by the presence of lawyers, first obtained following World
War II. However, legal assistance for an indigenous community did
not solve the many questions about rights and responsibilities con-
fronting individual Indians, including sales contracts, state and local
welfare, pawn, misdemeanors, and other pressing concerns. Creation
of the Navajo DNA People's Legal Services program in the 1960s
therefore had a dramatic effect on the lives of thousands of Navajos.

The creation of the Indian Claims Commission in 1946 prompted
the Navajos and many other Indian nations to gain legal counsel
for the first time. The Navajos chose between Norman Littell and
John Boyden. As did quite a few other Indian groups, the Navajo
Nation picked a person with extensive experience and current con-
nections with federal agencies in Washington, D.C. The current
Tribal Council chairman, Sam Ahkeah, opted for Littell. Boyden,
an attorney based in Salt Lake City, appeared before the Navajo
Tribal Council and expressed an interest in this position. But even

Exterior view of the Navajo Tribal Council chambers, with Window Rock in the distance.

though he knew some of the council delegates, that acquaintance did not make enough of a difference. Boyden then applied for the same position at the Hopi Nation, and this time around he got the job. He worked for the Hopis for a long time, but he never entirely got over his disappointment of having been passed over for the Navajo job.

Norman Littell held the position of general counsel for a generation. He helped transform the Navajo Tribal Council into a far more active and ambitious entity. In the initial decade following his assumption of duties as general counsel, he witnessed the council approve ten times as many resolutions as it had in the previous decade. Littell had been a Rhodes Scholar at Oxford University, and he did not mind being in the limelight. He was very involved in the early negotiations with the Peabody Coal Company and other coal companies. Bureau of Indian Affairs administrator Robert Young remembered: "When Littell thought he had worked out a really good deal for the tribe, he would come down the aisle in the chambers waving a piece of paper. He would be wearing a white suit. He really knew how to work that system, and he really was a powerful figure, especially in the 1950s."[1]

After his first ten years as general counsel, Littell said he had tried to achieve several goals: "[to guide] the Navajo leaders squarely to the legal positions on which they are entitled to stand as free American citizens . . . to throw a bridge across from an isolated society heretofore maintained deliberately as a matter of erroneous policy as a museum piece, to the broader life of American citizens in the world beyond their reservation to which they are rightfully entitled and to which they are rapidly attaining as full-fledged participants in the rich endowments of our free way of life."[2]

Nevertheless, both his first and final years were marked by confrontation and conflict. It cost the Navajo Nation to hire a lawyer, to maintain his office, and to cover his costs from Washington, D.C., to Window Rock. The Indian Claims Commission featured an ongoing bureaucratic process that moved at glacial speed. To some of the members of the Navajo Tribal Council, in particular delegate Annie Wauneka, it did not seem as though the Navajos were receiving very much in return for their investment.

By 1956, in her judgment, Littell had not shown he merited this kind of compensation. He proved to be sympathetic to development interests, but revealed little inclination to boost Navajo participation in the overall process. According to Wauneka, Littell needed to be more productive. "Now," she told the council, "when he tends to his job on the Claims Commission in behalf of the Navajo Tribe and gives us a specific instance at least one time showing us he is actually on the job and gives us some return on our hiring him to represent us on the Claims above, then we can get some assurance that . . . we have hired the right person to do a good job for us. So far he has not given us a definite showing and brought us some money here."

"Our attorney is a white man," Wauneka continued. "If we had an attorney from our own tribe to tell us these things which we have had told us by this white man, we would give it our hearty support, but there is a doubt of the present attorney's ability, or lack of it, to help us. . . . Now if we had some of our own law boys coming out of law school, I would have more faith in them."[3] Nevertheless, Littell influenced how the Navajo government functioned and what it could become. The Navajo government faced compelling issues during the years after World War II, and if it had not expanded its roles and responsibilities, county and state interests in Arizona,

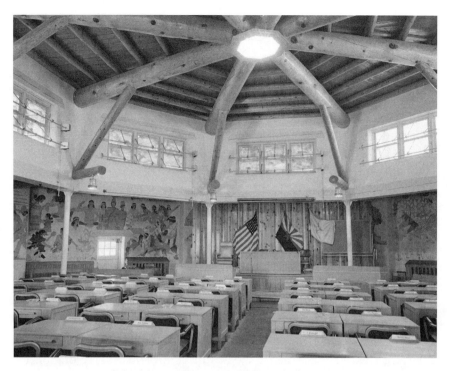

Interior view of the Navajo Tribal Council chambers.

New Mexico, and Utah would have wrested control or reinforced command over particular matters. With the rapid development of oil resources in Navajo country, the Navajo Tribal Council had new sources of income to fuel its expansion.

The establishment and expansion of the Navajo legal services program also have been enormously important. The consideration given to the program in this chapter provides a clear sense of how significant it became to the Navajo Nation and why it figured so prominently in Peterson Zah's life and career. Zah's enthusiasm for what the program tried to do and for what it achieved is quite evident. He names specific cases, cites the work of particular people, and stresses the importance of having Navajos becoming attorneys and "returning to the reservation to help their people." The DNA program also inspired more than a few Navajos to become law girls and law boys. This program constitutes an ongoing tribute to the ideas and ideals of Peterson Zah.

The Legacy of Littell

Zah: Norman Littell was there for a long time, and he's probably a typical general counsel for an Indian tribe. He was one powerful person for the Navajo Nation government. He created the office of general counsel with Navajo resources and was able to establish and expand his office so that it made his work a lot easier. He became a very powerful individual both here in Window Rock as well as in Washington, D.C.

The Navajo people like to see and talk to their tribal chairman in person. Norman Littell sometimes kept the Navajo people away from seeing their leader by saying that as legal counsel he needed to spend more time with the tribal chairman to discuss issues. He created a fearful atmosphere, and that's how he was able to control in Window Rock. Eventually he handled the Navajo–Hopi case against John Boyden of the Hopi. There's a lot of history between these two powerful individuals.

Littell also came to almost every Navajo Nation council session. He provided advice to the Navajo Nation council on every resolution before it was considered. He did not necessarily represent Navajo individuals. When some Navajo individuals wanted his representation, he just simply created the Navajo legal department and hired his own lawyers to be stationed at tribal headquarters in Window Rock.

If you look at Navajo history and their legal activities, Norman Littell's footprint is everywhere. In everything that the tribe did, whether that's leasing minerals, dealing with the coal companies, oil companies, water rights, and talking with huge corporations, Norman Littell had a big say in what the Navajo Nation Council did.

Iverson: He cast a long shadow. Littell's office was vitally important to the functioning of Navajo tribal government, but most individual Navajos would gain more attention in the 1960s with the establishment of the Navajo legal services program.

Zah: The first general counsel of the Navajo Nation was Norman Littell. As I understand Navajo history, he was really involved in what was going on in the Navajo Nation. He knew some of the leadership on the Navajo, as well as on the Hopi, reservation.

As I read some of the history of the Navajo people, Norman Littell, at one time, was really trying to have the Hopi tribal government

hire him as their lawyer. However, for some reason, it never really panned out.

It's ironic that, as I understand it, John Boyden was also doing the same thing. John Boyden was a well-known Hopi lawyer that handled the land case between Navajo and Hopi. He came over to the Navajo and knew some of the Navajo leadership just as well. And the two lawyers were jostling for position with these two tribes. And according to Annie Wauneka, John Boyden came to the Navajo Council one day and expressed interest in becoming the general counsel of the Navajo Nation. The Navajo council rejected his effort, and he became angry.

As soon as he walked out of the council chambers, he drove right over to the Hopi tribal council and told them about what happened, and they hired him. The Navajo people then had no choice except to now deal with Norman Littell. Because Norman Littell knew something about the land situation, too, that's how Norman Littell ended up working with the Navajo Nation.

Norman Littell's office was in Washington. Even though he was the general counsel to the Navajo Nation, he really did not have an office in Window Rock like many other lawyers who worked with Indian nations. He did have people that he relied on that were working for the Navajo government, and I think they were the ones that established the local Navajo legal department in Window Rock.

Iverson: That was fairly typical, wasn't it? There were a lot of lawyers who served and came out of the Wilkinson, Cragun & Barker firm and other similar firms. Boyden had the advantage of being relatively close by, living in Salt Lake City.

Zah: Yes. The general counsel was an entity and institution that outside companies had to go through to get to the chairman of the Tribal Council. On the Navajo Nation, he had certain things that he wanted to do, and he made sure that those things he wanted were done by the Navajo government. That kind of management of the tribal government really got people upset like Raymond Nakai, the former Navajo chairman. Nakai used this situation in his campaignings among the Navajo about how wrong it was to allow a white lawyer to become so powerful and involved in almost every aspect of our life. That was a rallying force to get Raymond Nakai elected in 1963.

Establishing the Navajo Legal Services Program

Zah: The federal Office of Economic Opportunity (OEO) included various services for the poor. The Navajo Nation applied to the OEO to establish a legal services program.

The DNA Legal Services program was very controversial from the very beginning. It was designed to help individuals who could not afford the services of an attorney. The Navajo community and the local people wanted to have an independent program free from political interference from tribal, state, and federal government. The people wanted honest legal opinion and to provide justice to cases they brought before the judicial forum.

We went to the local chapters and the five Navajo Agencies and explained the formation of a legal services program. Each chapter elected what they call a DNA representative to represent their inter-est from the 110 chapters throughout the Navajo Nation. Those representatives then became part of the agency council. There were five agency councils which met periodically to help the operation

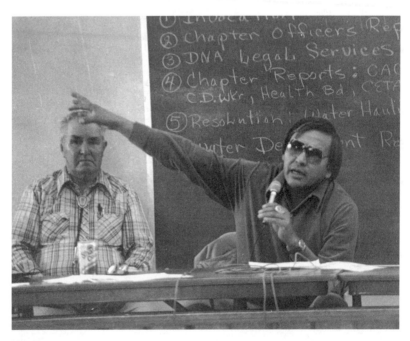

Peterson Zah at a meeting of the Navajo People's Legal Services program.

of the program. That group formed the board of directors for the Legal Services program. It became a very strong and powerful group rooted in Navajo communities.

Right from the beginning, many people started going to Legal Services attorneys for advice and for representation. They clashed with the establishment and officials in powerful positions, including the local public schools, the BIA agencies, and even with the agencies of the tribal government. In representing our clients we even had a dispute with the Navajo tribal court in the way they were set up—where the tribal judges are sometimes the prosecutor, counsel for defendants, advisor to inmates, etc.

The Navajo people really took pride in working with the Legal Services program. For the first time in their lives, they could seek the advice of lawyers on their particular situation. Many Navajo people bought vehicles and other household goods off the reservation. Some of these customers did not speak English very well, and they had to sign conditional sales contracts with car dealers. They didn't always understand the fine print in those contracts. As a result, the car dealers in many cases took advantage of the non-English-speaking customers. Some of our clients worked as labor for the coal companies and railroad seasonal migrant jobs.

Ted Mitchell Arrives

Zah: One day in 1967, I was teaching in a classroom here at ASU while working with and teaching VISTA volunteers. And I saw this one non-Indian person walking back and forth in the hallway. When the class ended, all the students left, and that guy came in. He didn't look familiar. I assumed that he was not from the Southwest or from Arizona because he was wearing a real loud tie and he had a nice suit. He was just a young man, maybe twenty-eight, thirty years old. He introduced himself as Theodore R. Mitchell, a lawyer from the Navajo Nation, and said, "I am a recent graduate of Harvard Law School. I actually went to high school here at Phoenix Union in Phoenix, Arizona, and I got my law degree from Harvard University just about eight months ago. I am starting a new legal services program with the Navajo Nation."

He continued by saying, "I am here to talk to you to see if I can convince you to come back to the Navajo." I told him I was happy here at ASU living with my family and liked working with the VISTA program. He explained the program and said, "Well, if you come back, here are some of the things that we want to do." We had our first conversation in the classroom, and then he ended by saying, "I'll come back some other time, because I've got a lot of business to do here in Phoenix."

A month later he came back. "Have you made up your mind? Have you thought about what I told you?" Ted Mitchell was very aggressive this time. I started thinking about what he was telling me and asked a lot of questions. He begged me, saying, "I really need your help. I need you in working with the Navajo people to start and complete the organization. Since you have the ability to talk both Navajo and English very well, you would be a great asset to the organization. You also have the experience of living here in Phoenix, where you know the non-Indian culture very well—I just really need that kind of a person to help me start this project." I was convinced and moved to Window Rock as an assistant to the director of the project.

At that time, the Legal Services program did not have a name. To the organization we added representatives from bar associations from the three states—Utah, Arizona, and New Mexico. These bar associations then selected a representative to the DNA People's Legal Services Board.

The Role of John Rockbridge

And so from those state and county bar associations and from the local agency council and chapters, we formed a board of directors. I remember one of the first meetings we had, we needed interpreters, because many of the Navajo people who got on the Legal Services Board did not speak English. And one particular person that was of interest to me was an elderly person. I believe he was about eighty years old at the time: John Rockbridge, who came from the Black Mesa area on the Navajo Nation. John was one of those individuals who was a tribal judge way back in the early and

late 1930s. He was a highly respected and very wise individual. And he became a member of the board of directors. We put a headphone on his ears, and I was his interpreter during the proceedings of the meeting.

The naming of the legal services program was the first item on the agenda, followed by how it should be organized. Its bylaws also had to be adopted. The naming of the legal services program, I thought, was going to be just a simple, maybe five-minute discussion. But I was wrong. It took about two to three hours. We had a long debate on several proposed names. Finally, John Rockbridge rose at the board meeting, and he said, "I would like to speak to the issue." He explained very eloquently what went on in his mind as the discussion took place and as he listened to the debate. He said, "I want to make a motion in naming this Legal Services program board, and I want to call it Diné Bee'iiná' Náhiilnah Bee Agha'diit'aahii." And everybody kind of chuckled, and they said, "Mr. Zah, you now have to interpret all of that into English."

Iverson: What did Mr. Rockbridge say?

Zah: And what it really meant was "Diné" is the people. "Bee'iiná" is the culture. "Náhiilnah" is revitalization. What John had in the name was, why don't we call this program the Navajo People's Program. And the cultural revitalization—that's what we're trying to do. Lawyers—Bee Agha'diit'aahii means its lawyers. And that's the way John explained it, so we named the program Diné Bee'iiná' Náhiilnah Bee Agha'diit'aahii. John's motion carried, and that's how the program got its name. It was through an elderly, wise individual who had a lot of experience in working with the cases that came before Navajo courts.

I always admired John Rockbridge for his wisdom and advice he provided. When he appeared in federal courts with us, I was always his interpreter. I learned a tremendous amount about Navajo values, culture, language, and the behavioral pattern of the elderly people, and even learning how to speak publicly, and the protocol that one has to go through at Navajo meetings. I helped John by interpreting for him. But I also learned so much from him. And he had a good sense of humor at the same time. John lived to be over ninety years old, until we lost him in the late 1970s. He was an outstanding spokesman for the Navajo people. He always had some wise things

to say. He didn't say much throughout the day, but when he decided to open his mouth and talk, I always tell young people, you better listen. Because he doesn't always talk, but when he does, there are some good lessons to be learned.

That's how the program was named. We were getting something like, at the beginning, several million dollars a year from the OEO legal services program. That enabled us to hire about thirty lawyers, about thirty tribal court advocates with supportive staff. The advocates were lay advocates who practiced law in the Navajo Nation courts. The thing that was also intriguing to me was when I asked the program director Ted Mitchell if we had money from the Office of Economic Opportunity for the building of the offices. We didn't have any office space. I said, "Where are we going to get an office facility? We've got to have an office in all the five agencies throughout the Navajo Nation." And Ted just listened, smiled a little, and said, "Mr. Zah, that's why I hired you. You figure all that out," and "If you can't find them, create them. You build the office, because you're a carpenter." And he would say, "I remember looking at your resume—you're a journeyman carpenter, so you should just help me build those offices."

Recruiting and Hiring Lawyers

I went to the Navajo Forest Products Industry, a tribal program. They were the people who had the sawmill established in Navajo, New Mexico. They were cutting trees and hauling in logs, and they were producing lumber. And I used to go to them for some lumber and donation. The Navajo Forest Products Industry was always kind enough to work with us to build the badly needed office spaces. On occasion we used program funds to buy these materials.

We put all of the thirty lawyers and associates into those offices to begin working on their cases. I remember when we opened those offices we would have a grand opening and the reception room would be just full of clientele—people ready to see lawyers, to see tribal court advocates. It was something that was really amazing to me, how the program was greatly received and supported by the local people.

Many of the thirty non-Indian lawyers did not have much experience. I think we hired two or three experienced lawyers, out of Phoenix and Farmington and Albuquerque. And their job was just to work with the inexperienced lawyers that recently came out of the law school.

One of my responsibilities was to recruit or hire lawyers and advocates. In our budget, we had a position for lawyers that we were supposed to have on staff. Well, out on the Navajo reservation, you don't have lawyers walking the streets looking for jobs.

You had to be innovative in ways to get lawyers to your program. So every year, I packed up my bags, my toothbrushes, my clothes, and I and a lawyer would start out at Boston University, Harvard University, Yale, NYU, American University in Washington, D.C., John Marshall in Chicago. And I would comb the whole country for ten days, two weeks at a time during the year. I would keep a profile on all of the first-, second-, and third-year students. And the ones that we liked, I'd bring them out to the DNA Legal Services program during the summer to clerk for us. They were the law clerks, working with experienced lawyers. We did that for a long time.

We talked to all the students that were interested in legal services. And we managed to get enough funds to bring them out during the summer. They clerked for us. I remember when the legal services program became so controversial that the federal government was having difficulty in deciding where to put us in the federal system. As a result, the federal government created an independent Legal Services Corporation. That entity was to be separate and apart from all the other programs. And that's when we started working with the newly established Legal Services Corporation Board. I remember when people like Hillary Rodham were nominated by President Jimmy Carter to serve on the board. From the American Indian community, we all recommended Dick Trudell, from the Berkeley, California, area. He became our representative. Cecilia Esquer, an ASU law graduate, was also a board member. That's how I got to know some of these people. And that was even before Hillary Rodham married Bill Clinton.

In the early 1970s, our service area expanded to include Hopi, Apache, and all the indigent poor in the Four Corners area. This caused the Legal Service Corporation to increase our funds. And DNA thus became one of the largest legal services program in

America. It had a lot of spunk and excitement. Because it was doing a lot of good things, it attracted some excellent lawyers to the program.

Because it was a free legal service, we had a lot of Indian people that just came to see us. Our offices were always full, including people with a divorce problem; employment discrimination; discrimination experienced in the cities; land problems; problems with their Social Security; problems with them being fired by the tribal government; BIA; Indian Health Service; maybe even a malpractice case at Indian Health Service. At the height of the program, it was not unusual to have DNA handle over twelve thousand cases a year.

Legal Reform Units

An outstanding feature of DNA People's Legal Services that I really liked was the creation of what we call a law reform unit. The unit was staffed with the most experienced working out of our office handling and litigating major-impact law reform cases. These cases were carefully selected and litigated in tribal, state, and federal courts. The goal was to win those cases, and they would set precedent and have major impacts on the lives of people.

It was an important feature. We had some of the great trial lawyers helping us with those cases. And we took some of those cases to the U.S. Supreme Court. One of them was the *McClanahan* case in the state of Arizona, where Rosalind McClanahan questioned the taxation of the state of Arizona on her income while she lived and worked on the Navajo Nation. Her income was generated by a local reservation entity. The U.S. Supreme Court ruled that Ms. McClanahan, since she had her allegiance to the Navajo Nation government and she is stationed on the Navajo reservation, she wasn't obligated to pay state income taxes.

That case became a decision that enhanced tribal sovereignty. To me, it reinforced our sovereignty and gave us a shot in the arm to start the tribal sovereignty movement throughout the Indian nation. Subsequent to *McClanahan*, other similar cases were brought before the federal courts, and some worked their way up to the U.S. Supreme Court as well.

Iverson: Could you name two or three accomplishments or achievements or areas where you think you made significant headway during this time?

Zah: To begin with, there were just too many cases that we were involved in. The whole program was amazing. The cases that went to the Supreme Court, at the top of the list was probably the *McClanahan* case. And the second one is the revamping of the Apache County in northern Arizona. The redistricting of Apache County was done by court order. And as a result, Apache County had to expand its services to include offices in Ganado, and then one in Chinle, on the Navajo reservation.

Iverson: As opposed to just having one in St. Johns?

Zah: As opposed to having one office off the reservation in St. Johns.

Iverson: Considerably off the reservation.

Zah: Fully controlled by the non-Indians.

Iverson: Yes, a mere 135 miles south of Chinle.

One Person, One Vote

Zah: DNA was able to assist in the restructuring of the county voting district to follow the one man–one vote mandated by the federal election laws. Apache County is a long rectangle-shaped county that extends into the Navajo reservation and St. Johns, Arizona, off-reservation. The state courts helped divide the county into three equal parts based on population and voting districts.

The third one that's very important was to obtain a court order that created in Arizona and New Mexico the construction of high schools on the Navajo Nation. In Arizona there was Window Rock High School. But Window Rock High School was not really a legally instituted high school. It was an elementary school district teaching high school subjects fully controlled by Apache County off-reservation. The state never declared it a high school on the Navajo reservation. The legal status of high schools being built on the Navajo reservation always brought a lot of discussion among education leaders, at least in Arizona. This situation had to be changed, and we were looking for ways to do it.

We brought a case called *Natonabah* before the state of New Mexico. Gallup–McKinley County School District had the only major high school in McKinley County. They were busing Navajo children from communities on the Navajo reservation into Gallup for hours to come to school, and then at the end of the day take them back to their home communities. Well, if you did that to students, they were unable to participate in any kind of athletic, extracurricular activity at the school, because they spent all of their time riding back and forth. And so you had to wonder about, when do these kids learn? When do they do their homework? How long are they in class?

Iverson: Even in areas where the Navajos formed a majority on a school board, they still confronted transportation problems. The Chinle school district, for example, is the size of Connecticut.

Zah: The *Natonabah* case involved the issue of Gallup-McKinley schools misusing federal funds appropriated to them to use to advance the education of Indian children that required special and unique attention. The case was litigated in federal district court in Albuquerque, New Mexico, along with the application of the Indian Self-Determination Act in the contracting of schools by local Indian communities. This case was instrumental in the building of new schools in Navajo communities close to the students' homes on the Navajo reservation. The DNA lawyers only used Gallup–McKinley County School District as an example to equalize funding so there wouldn't be any need for busing students from faraway places. As a result, schools were built at Tohatchi, Newcomb, Crownpoint, and at Navajo, and Ramah, New Mexico. The Indian Self-Determination Act was an impetus to local control of schools at Rough Rock, Ramah, Rock Point, and at many Indian communities in Indian country.

I remember interpreting in a similar case in Utah when a federal judge in Salt Lake City made the comment, "When do they study if they go out into the highway at 5:00 a.m., 5:30 in the morning to catch a bus, and then go to school all day and get back on the bus at 3:30 to go home? It might be snowing, and you let them off the bus at those highways, aren't you really jeopardizing the safety of those children?"

In Utah, it was because of the *Tsinnijinnie* case that the schools on-reservation were built, and because of that, the birth of Monument Valley High School and Whitehorse High School, and now the

Navajo Mountain High School. It was mandated by the courts. Utah and San Juan County are still carrying out the spirit of the judge's decision and mandate.

So the *Natonabah* case was developed in such a way that it would create new schools. And that went to court, and court-ordered schools were created. So a judge had to order the state and the federal government that they should have these schools, these institutions, out in the Navajo communities. And in both of these cases the defense by the state was that "it's too expensive." However, it didn't mean much to the judges.

Iverson: Yes. It's always too expensive.

Zah: "It's too expensive." But the judge says, "We're not talking about expense here. We are talking about equality and fairness in education. We're talking about making opportunities available. Treating everybody equally that's within your school district. And you've got to extend these facilities to the Navajo people." To me these were also major-impact cases.

Iverson: And it meant Intermountain could close?

Zah: That caused the Intermountain boarding school in Brigham City, Utah, and many of the other off-reservation boarding schools to close. And the federal government said, "Since they have schools now on the reservation, we're going to close these boarding schools in Phoenix, California, Utah, and Oklahoma. And we're going to bring all those kids home, and they will now go to schools in local communities on the Navajo Nation."

Seeking Solutions

Those were the kind of legal cases DNA was involved in which made the program highly controversial. DNA employees didn't invent those cases. They didn't scheme and connive as to which agency we should go after. We were pushed by our clients. The Navajo people wanted solutions to their problems.

And the last one I'll just mention is a case against the Navajo Nation Council, where the issue of reapportionment was raised by a Navajo client from Shiprock, New Mexico. And his question was very simple, where he said: "If you closely examine the Navajo

Council delegate seats, we have a situation where a delegate from the LeChee chapter in the Western agency chapter represents about two hundred constituents. And he is responsible for one chapter house. A council delegate that represents Shiprock represents several thousand people. But when both vote on issues in the council, their votes weigh the same. Where's equality? Where's fairness? What does the law say?" And they wanted us to handle that case immediately and before the upcoming election.

We sued the Navajo Council in the *Yazzie* case, demanding reapportionment of voting districts to reflect equal representation and the one man–one vote theory. That really turned the Tribal Council against us. The council then started raising questions about DNA activities, and some suggested even the defunding of the program. However, the Navajo Nation has an equal protection and representation clause in the Navajo Bill of Rights. So it was our own Navajo law on fairness and equal representation that got the *Yazzie* case into the Navajo courts.

On the federal side, there was the United States Civil Rights Act that mandated the same sentiment. The United States Senate and House of Representatives got into the act by amending the Economic Opportunity Act to curtail the activities of the Legal Services program. I remember a book entitled *All the President's Men*. There is some mention that Senator Barry Goldwater of Arizona was complaining about DNA Legal Services getting into too many social issues in Arizona. The conversation took place between President Nixon, two Arizona congressmen, and Senator Goldwater on a flight from Washington to Phoenix. The reporter wrote about how legal services programs nationwide should be completely eliminated.

Using the Judicial System

Zah: We were using the judicial system to resolve problems clients brought to us. But at the same time, we urged our clients to educate their peers and organize them around those issues. The people have to be involved with what is going on in court—because you don't

want to go to court all by yourself as a lawyer; there have to be simultaneous movements to create social change in the communities. These movements have to complement one another, so when you win the case, it means something to the people.

Another way of bringing long-term changes is by challenging and motivating people to take their own responsibility and solving problems. At this point, we didn't have a single Navajo lawyer. One day it dawned on me, and I said, "What am I doing here? We have a lot of non-Indian lawyers working for us across the reservation, trying to change our institutions and defend us. Maybe we should try growing our own Navajo lawyers."

In 1969, we systematically began planting seeds and cultivating some interest among the youth to become lawyers. We went to every high school on the Navajo Nation and encouraged students to stay in school and produce good grades which will create opportunities to college and to law school. DNA established a scholarship fund using gifts from foundations, bar associations, and interested people from the private sector. The Navajo Nation also provided scholarship funds to undergraduate students. In the late 1970s, we began noticing students finding their way to law schools throughout the Southwest. We would employ those law students during the summer as clerks and assisting attorneys with their cases. The program became highly successful as these students began graduating from law school, coming back to the reservation and becoming staff attorneys, judges, prosecutors, and one even became a state legislator in Arizona.

Navajo Attorneys

Iverson: Who were several of the significant Navajo attorneys?

Zah: I will name a few of them. One of them was Claudeen Bates Arthur, from the Shiprock area, who ultimately became a director of litigation at DNA, and I appointed her as the first attorney general for the Navajo Nation in 1983. Then she also became the first woman chief justice of the Navajo Nation Supreme Court. Claudeen was one of those individuals that we worked with at an early age to get her interested and started in law, because she was so bright.

Actually, she became an institution on the Navajo, with that genera-
tion of the Navajo people. She was my favorite person and a good
practicing lawyer who helped argue the *Kerr-McGee* case in the U.S.
Supreme Court and was highly respected and admired by many.

The other one was Herbert Yazzie who came out of Kayenta,
Arizona. I also appointed him as attorney general, and now he is the
chief justice of the Navajo Nation. He is presently doing a remark-
able job in administering justice. Both Claudeen and Herb Yazzie
went to law school here at ASU. They were two of the first Native
American students to graduate from law school and pass the state
bar. They were both pioneers in growing our own lawyers, returning
to the Navajo reservation to help their people.

And then there is Louis Denetsosie, the current attorney general
of the Navajo Nation. These were representatives of Navajo people
who stepped forward to address the concern in producing more
young Navajo people interested in law. I liked that feature of the
DNA program because it was different, new and challenging. Legal
Services program rules were flexible enough to allow for these kinds
of innovative initiatives. A legal services official in Washington, D.C.,
asked questions about our activities in schools, and we just explained
how something like this was a necessity. Our clients demanded such
action. This initiative produced about twenty Navajo lawyers within
a fifteen-year period. That's progress, a big, huge progress, probably
more important than cases DNA handled and won in court. That
was close to my heart while working at DNA. It has a major impact
on the life of the Navajo Nation and on the Navajo. This was an
extraordinary effort that had a major impact on the Navajo people.

Iverson: Was Tom Tso part of that?

Zah: Tom Tso was the first chief justice of the newly established
Navajo Supreme Court in 1985. He used to work with us at DNA
Legal Services.

I'm very proud to say that DNA just celebrated its fortieth anni-
versary this past summer. The program is still running, operating
smoothly, and is still representing a significant number of clients in
the Four Corners area as well as on the Hopi and Apache reservations.

Some of the American Indian students that come to ASU law
school say they got their interest in law because of what they saw and

experienced at DNA People's Legal Services program. That was the goal of the program right from the beginning, to create that kind of atmosphere among the Indian people here in the Southwest.

Iverson: Because DNA has been here for forty years, it means, especially for younger people, a lot of these things are new to them. They weren't there when Mrs. Wauneka had that confrontation with Ted Mitchell, and a variety of other things. So I think your ability to give a firsthand kind of perspective on this is really important.

Zah: In the 1960s, Ted Mitchell, the first director of the DNA Legal Services program, also came into the picture. I remember lots of discussions among tribal employees how this white lawyer became so powerful. Ted Mitchell was a civil libertarian who believed in individual rights and representation of individual Navajos. He supported civil rights and promoted the freedom to do whatever one wishes as long as they do not break the law. He got involved with the Native American Church, which was not popular at the time with tribal leadership and their general counsel.

Through Norman Littell's urging, the Navajo Council passed a resolution suggesting that the Navajo people should not join the Native American Church. He argued, "You have your own religion here on the Navajo, and you are sovereign and can dictate religious preference." All this was said and done in the early and late 1950s before the passage of the Navajo Bill of Rights and the federal Indian Civil Rights Act.

Well, Ted Mitchell came along, and he said, "Norman Littell is wrong. You have freedom of religion just like anywhere else in America. You're free to believe whatever you want to believe in." And so immediately there was a clash between two lawyers that developed into a huge controversy on the Navajo reservation.

Native American Church

Iverson: Painter R. C. Gorman liked to observe that all the major components of Navajo culture had been stolen and improved upon. The ability of the Navajos to incorporate new elements into their culture has been demonstrated again and again. Livestock,

silversmithing, and basketball are cases in point. The Native American Church furnished a severe test of that capacity to bring in and incorporate a new institution.

The Native American Church originated outside of Navajo country, but it provided a source for brotherhood and for dealing with alcoholism. Many traditional Navajos opposed the introduction of this alternative religion. Many scorned it because of its employment of peyote, but over time its value emerged for many members of the Navajo Nation, and eventually the Native American Church became a significant element in modern Navajo life.

Zah: Well, the Native American Church movement, I guess, happened way back sometime in the late 1930s, 1940s. And the Native American people had their own way of practicing their religious beliefs and what they believe in. I don't know all of the details and I don't pretend to be a historian on the subject, but that's something that the Navajo people felt, going into the mid-1950s, when this movement came to the Navajo Nation. And many of the Navajo people—who, by the way, went to school—they went to school in Oklahoma, they went to school in other places throughout America, and they became friends in contact with other Indian tribes that had that religion. And they intermarried with some of those other Indian tribal members, and that whole idea of the Native American Church movement then began moving on to the Navajo Nation. And I remember the Navajo Nation government fought them. And they even passed a resolution—a Tribal Council resolution—saying that, you know, they don't really belong on the Navajo Nation. So in many respects, it was discriminatory, using religion for the Navajo Nation to do what they did.

But the Navajo Nation, being a sovereign nation, the courts left it alone. And the Native American Church—people were raising the issue of freedom of religion, spelled out in the United States Constitution. So that battle began way back then.

There's one individual, David Clark, who really lived through this whole fight between the tribal government and the Native American Church. David Clark is considered one of the top leaders in the Native American Church, and lives on the Navajo to this day. He still makes his home in Teesto, Arizona. He is a highly respected individual, very bright individual, and really loves the Navajo people. And I have a tremendous amount of respect for David for what he

believes and for what he did as an individual to enhance and to make the Church a lot stronger around the Navajo.

Some people may disagree with the Native American Church. But it's a religion; it's a belief. It's a belief. They have every right to promote what they were promoting. But one of the things that caught my eye as a young boy was what they were teaching. They were teaching that, for example, drinking is wrong. They were teaching that you can't do all of these violent things against one another, that if you have children, you have to take care of your children. And that education was very important. They talked—the local people, all these, for me, wonderful things, because I heard them say that. And because of that, I guess early on, I decided that, you know, if they are promoting all of those things, then why are we fighting?

And it was no different than my also listening to, for example, a church such as the Protestants or the Catholics doing the same thing out there. And they were teaching some good things.

The Native American Church was a big movement that was pushed by individuals like David Clark. And there was another person by the name of Hola Tso. He was from around the Sawmill area that lived through a lot during that period of time. And he worked very closely with David Clark. David Clark was just a young man. David Clark was this individual that got jailed and arrested by tribal police and got jail. But he never gave in. He just kept on going and kept on going. And that's why he's such a devoted person to the Church, is because of what he went through. And to this day he's still considered one of the well-known American Indian religious leaders throughout America. He certainly has my respect for some of the things that he did accomplish; he accomplished a lot.

Some say that probably around half of the Navajo Nation is a member of the Native American Church, or some would say, no, it's really a third. You have one-third of the Navajo people that belong to the Native American Church; one-third that still believes in the Navajo tradition; another third that believes in Christianity. And so they're out there. And they are groups to be reckoned with.

Iverson: It's really one of the major achievements of your time in Navajo political life, it seems to me. When we talked about DNA Legal Services, we talked about Ted Mitchell, and we talked about other people who were involved. One thing we didn't talk directly

about was that important confrontation that took place between Mrs. Wauneka and Mr. Mitchell that ended up with Mr. Mitchell having to move his offices from the Navajo Nation to Gallup, New Mexico. This incident also had an impact on the present and future leadership of DNA. There's a lot of mythology at this point, and lots of guesses and suppositions, but they are not necessarily accurate.

Zah: Well, I don't really completely remember that day, because I was not at the office. I may have been at another agency office, like Chinle or Shiprock, or doing something away from Window Rock when all of that happened. But as I talked to people who were there that day, there was a lot of discussion by the Navajo Council on this Indian Civil Rights Act that had been passed recently by Congress.

Indian Civil Rights Act

In 1968, the Indian Civil Rights Act was attached to a major congressional bill. And there was one section about "providing due process to any person," and the Navajo Council was concerned with that section. Does providing due process within the Navajo Nation context mean that "any person" besides a Navajo, or "any person" from the Navajo Nation? What does it mean we have to "provide due process to any person"? What about tourists? What about all these other people? And if we do incarcerate or arrest somebody, how much due process should be given to those individuals? That kind of a discussion generated a lot of talks among the lawyers, because naturally, they were defending the civil rights and the rights of Navajo Nation, Hopi, and Apaches, and what that all meant within the context of tribal governments.

Ted Mitchell, the director of DNA Legal Services, was naturally interested, because there was a lot of discussion about his activities on the Navajo Nation, and getting involved in a lot of issues that the Navajo Nation was confronting. And there were water rights issues, there were land issues, there were issues with the Tribal General Counsel, the lawyers that represented the whole Navajo Nation and their activities.

There were a lot of questions about schools out in the communities, and some of the events and activities that those schools were,

I guess, involved in relative to students, and not giving them due process and violating their rights. I think right at that point, there was a lot of discussion about long hair, the long-hair issue where if a Navajo youngster wants to participate in football, the football coaches were causing them to have their haircuts first before they joined the football team. It didn't matter whether that person had skills or not, was being athletic or not. And so that all involved the civil rights matters of that individual. Naturally, their lawyers were very much interested.

Wauneka Punches Out Mitchell

As I understand it, that day Ted Mitchell went over to the Navajo Council along with two or three other lawyers. And so they were sitting there in the Navajo Council when an individual from the Department of Interior, from the solicitor's office, came out to explain the new law. When they came to that section on providing due process to anyone, to non-Indians, there was a lot of contention, a lot of emotions involved. I guess the council tried not to name anybody, but Ted Mitchell knew that he was the center of that discussion. He thought it was funny why they wouldn't name him, but he knew clearly that whatever was said, that was him. He thought that was funny. And so he ended up laughing about the matter, and I guess at one point, another question was asked, and that made him laugh really hard, and everybody heard it in the council. Annie Wauneka was one of those individual council delegates that sat in the very back row, because the council seats were assigned in the alphabetical order.

Since her last name was "Wauneka," she was near the back, sitting with the Yazzies and the Yellowhairs. She just got out of her chair from that last row, because Ted Mitchell was right in back of her. Maybe Ted Mitchell thought that she was going to leave, that she was ready to leave or something like that, and didn't pay much attention to how angry she was. And when Ted was looking away, he didn't see this punch coming from Annie Wauneka, and Annie Wauneka punched him in the mouth. That caused a lot of controversy throughout the reservation. DNA People's Legal Service ended up suing the tribal government. The chairman of the Navajo

tribe, Raymond Nakai, sent police over to DNA, and the police then escorted Ted Mitchell towards Gallup, and left him at the reservation line. He had to walk some distance. Maybe he hitchhiked into Gallup. Then he was instructed not to set foot back on the Navajo Nation.

In the Navajo Treaty of 1868, there is also a section dealing with "bad men among the Indians." The United States government or the tribal government can expel a "bad man" from Indian land, and drive him off the reservation. The Navajo Nation used that section of the treaty to get Ted Mitchell off the reservation.

The Indian Civil Rights Act of 1968 said that you had to give due process to anyone, "any person," and the legal issue for the judge and the court to decide was the difference between those two. Ted Mitchell eventually won. The court decided that his civil rights had been violated. Sometime later he returned to the Navajo Nation to resume his duty as the executive director of DNA People's Legal Service.

Iverson: But he really couldn't in some ways, could he? He was really sort of a marked man. It made it harder for him to carry on as he carried on before.

Zah: At that point, Ted Mitchell thought that he was distracting his employees and what DNA was all about and making it harder for DNA to achieve its goals. He elected to move to Hawaii and serve there as a legal aid program director. From Hawaii he went on to Micronesia, where he served for many years as its legal services director.

As a young man and still in college, I used to go to those council sessions and listen to the debates. A lot of the debates revolved around civil rights versus the tribal government rights. And for me that was so interesting and exciting as I was learning a lot.

All of the arguments from both sides caused a lot of fireworks. Raymond Nakai and his forces in the council voted not to renew Littell's contract. It was something that was quite significant among the Navajo people to see it happen soon after the inauguration. During Raymond Nakai's first term, the Navajo Bill of Rights was passed and considered one of his biggest accomplishments of his administration.

Iverson: Nakai initially was very positive about DNA Legal Services. Over time, however, there were some issues that developed, and he became less supportive.

Zah: Yes. I believe that it was right at the beginning of the Legal Services program in 1968 when Ted Mitchell also became an advocate of Navajo water rights. All the research on the subject pointed subsequent court decisions toward the concept that Indian tribes have prior water rights, that the Navajo government should not be giving those water rights away to local municipalities, power plants, and farming industry. Ted Mitchell was saying the water is badly needed on the Navajo reservation.

MacDonald and the Office of Navajo Economic Opportunity

Raymond Nakai's administration introduced Peter MacDonald to the Navajo people. Peter MacDonald had just returned to the Navajo Nation from Los Angeles where he used to work for Hughes Aircraft Company as an engineer.

Raymond Nakai needed a lot of help in reorganizing the tribal government and to start new programs. With the beginning of the War on Poverty programs nationwide, the Navajo Nation elected to participate in these programs and created the Office of Navajo Economic Opportunity [ONEO], through which it could apply for those funds as a quasi-independent tribal entity.

Raymond Nakai then appointed Peter MacDonald as the director of the newly established Office of Navajo Economic Opportunity. And so when that happened, many, many Navajo people became employed by the ONEO program. Some of them were very, very popular, like the Head Start program. It meant jobs for Navajo people, and it was a program that employed individuals that were otherwise not able to find work on the Navajo reservation. And they were doing some good things, too. Such as the community development program, and the home improvement program—people's homes were being renovated, and some were building new homes, new houses. Those became very, very popular with the Navajo people, because it was for the first time providing services to the local people. People were feeling the impact of some of those services, and as a result, Peter MacDonald became very popular.

Raymond Nakai and Peter MacDonald as political allies, following
MacDonald's successful campaign to succeed Nakai.

From that position he then ran for the tribal chairmanship against
his old friend Raymond Nakai. I think they ran against each other
about three times during the course of the next twelve, sixteen years.
They dominated the political scene on the Navajo Nation.

Iverson: I was curious about your initial impressions of Peter
MacDonald. With DNA initially under the umbrella of the ONEO,

you must have had some meetings or contacts with him and had an initial impression of him.

Zah: I guess the best way to describe that is that because of the programs that we were responsible for—with my helping the development of the DNA People's Legal Services, and with Mr. MacDonald being the head of ONEO—those jobs, things that the two programs were doing to force us to work together. Because the program demanded it. My impression was that he was an able, capable person, and an individual that was looking out for the interests of the Navajo people. He wanted to make sure that whatever it was that we would do was in the best interests of our individual clients. And he represented the Navajo Nation as its young-and-upcoming leader, and he was always interested in some of the things that DNA was doing in education and economic development.

Back then he supported the Legal Services program. And we needed his support at the time because the Navajo Nation government was trying to cut us off. The Navajo Tribal Council, controlled by Raymond Nakai, was passing resolutions, saying things about the Legal Services program, what we shouldn't be doing and why we shouldn't do certain things.

Well, Mr. MacDonald saw things a little differently than the way the Tribal Council did. He came to our defense, to save the program and the project. That kind of forced us to work together as individuals representing those two important entities on the Navajo Nation.

Iverson: You weren't entirely surprised that he decided to run in 1970 for the chairman's position.

Zah: I wasn't surprised. Because when you get into those positions, you go through a process that makes it more likely that you will become a serious candidate to be the chairman of the Navajo Nation.

5

Traders

"They Were the Bank, the Post Office, the Loan Office, and the Employment Agency"

UNTIL RATHER RECENTLY, MOST ACCOUNTS relating to trading posts focused primarily on the years prior to 1950 and the major figures of this earlier period, including J. L. Hubbell, Thomas Keam, and J. B. Moore. Family members or longtime friends often fashioned these depictions. It is not entirely surprising these overviews tended to portray traders in the best possible light. However, the more recent period confronted chroniclers with a very different scene. Navajos began to acquire motor vehicles, and they drove these vehicles at unprecedented speeds on newly paved roads right past the old mom-and-pop-style posts and into town.

After the imposition of livestock reduction, fewer sheep inevitably meant fewer rugs. If Navajos went to Gallup or another border town, they might be headed there less to seek higher prices for their weaving than lower prices for everything from Pepsi to potato chips. Even the old posts that had figured prominently in the weaving business saw their market diminished. A place like Shonto might benefit slightly from an upsurge in the 1970s in the Navajo pottery market in the nearby Cow Springs community, but by this time Shonto appeared to be renting more videotapes than it was selling textiles.

A closer look at the history of trading posts, in fact, yields a more complicated story. Reports from the Navajo Nation well

before World War II provided specific instances of violent behavior against Navajos by several traders. Many Navajos continued to complain about attitudes and business practices. Anthropologist William Y. Adams, in his classic study of Shonto published by the Bureau of American Ethnology in 1963,[1] called the connection a kind of parent-child relationship with clear lines drawn in regard to Navajo responses to trader paternalism. Following World War II, encouraged and emboldened by general counsel Norman Littell, the Navajo Tribal Council began to push for a review of how the posts conducted business. In 1948, Tribal Council members Dewey Etsitty and Roger Davis complained about traders paying limited rent or no money at all in order to do business in Navajo country.[2] Although the traders escaped major changes, the door to real change had at last been opened.

The transition began with what Chemehuevi attorney Fred Ragsdale called "the first modern Indian law case." *Williams v. Lee* (1959) concerned a non-Indian trader who sued in state court in order to collect foods sold on credit. The U.S. Supreme Court reversed the decision of the Arizona Supreme Court, with Justice Hugo Black concluding: "There can be no doubt that to allow state jurisdiction here would undermine the authority of the tribal courts over reservation affairs and hence would infringe on the right of the Indians to govern themselves."[3]

In the 1960s, the number of trading posts declined from 137 to 100, with 17 of the posts operated by Navajos. The establishment of the Navajo DNA Legal Services program in the 1960s followed *Williams v. Lee* with an insistence at the local level necessary to forge lasting change. The newly minted lawyers Peterson Zah recruited for the Legal Services program tended to be young, adamant, and persistent. They sued various traders for the way in which they did business, and they were able to get the Federal Trade Commission to launch a formal investigation into contemporary business practices. Public hearings held in Chinle, Crownpoint, Kayenta, Pinon, Shiprock, Tuba City, and Window Rock in the summer of 1972 and new rules and regulations underlined the obvious: a new day had dawned.

Because of the power enjoyed by trading post operators for decades and the kind of monopolies they had held in many parts of

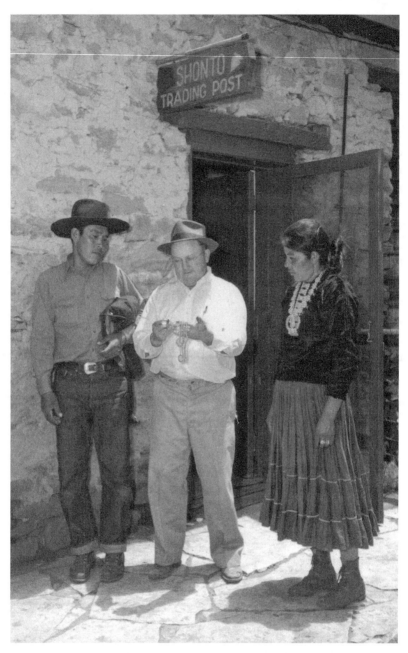

A trader at the Shonto Trading Post examines the work of a Navajo silversmith. The post was established in 1913. It helped expand the market for the work of Navajo artists.

Navajo country, the traders were not prepared culturally or financially for major changes imposed on how they did business. Their plummeting position would have become progressively more evident, but they were not prepared for their version of stock reduction.

It remained convenient for the traders and their allies to try to ignore or discredit the indictment the young lawyers had so carefully and shrewdly crafted. But as Zah's recollections remind and instruct us, this transition could not be ignored. Not too long ago one could not have imagined major change in this world. As Zah phrases it so powerfully, the trader had been the bank, the post office, the loan office, and the employment agency. Practically and symbolically, the trading post system furnished a vital test for the DNA Legal Services program. The victories that DNA realized in regard to gaining greater authority over trading post practices represented a crucial step in what Zah presents as an ongoing battle by the Navajos for greater self-determination.

Going to the Trading Post

Zah: I was still a young man when one day my dad told me that he wanted me to go with him to the Keams Canyon Trading Post. I would say it's a good ten-mile ride. My dad saddled up the horse early in the morning light before sunrise. And I sat in the back, and we rode into Keams Canyon on the way to work. He was working in the coal mine there, right below Keams Canyon on the west side of the trading post.

When we got to the store that day I had my first sight of a white trader. I couldn't understand what they were saying, because they were speaking English, and I didn't know one word of English by then. I thought these are the people that offer some goods to the Navajo people for a price. They're the people who exercise a lot of power by controlling the prices of the commodities at the trading post. I thought back then that it was probably only for those people that they liked.

I was just a young kid no taller than the counter where my dad was doing the trading. My dad wanted to buy some food that could

In the era when few Navajos owned motor vehicles, the time-honored wagon served as a major means of transportation.

A truck burdened with sacks of wool heads out from the Lukachukai Trading Post in 1947.

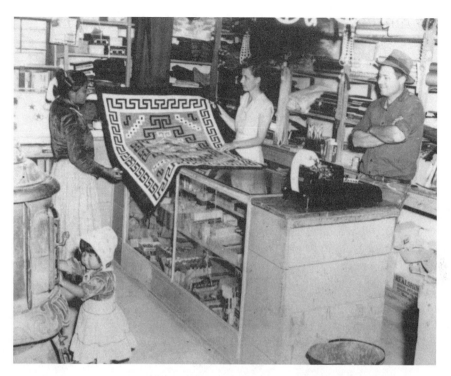

A Navajo weaver attempts to make a sale to Bessie and Melvin McGee at the Tocito Trading Post in 1955, Tocito, New Mexico, near Sanostee, New Mexico.

last him for a week there at the coal mine, and my job was to get a sack of flour and maybe potatoes and coffee and put them on the saddle and take them back to my mother and sisters back home. So that was my first sight of a white man. It was quite an experience, and I was afraid that they might drag me off to school.

I didn't really get to know any of them well because our family really didn't have the money to continue visiting the trading post. I just stayed away from them. And I think the second time that I went back to the trading post was when I was on my way to school at Tuba City. This was in the late 1940s. I had to catch the mail truck from the trading post to get back to school and home in Low Mountain. And in some cases, they were helpful. But at the same time, they were doing a lot of businesslike activities within that community.

I didn't really get to learn more about what they were into until I went to college and I came back. I had been a deputy director of DNA People's Legal Services for about a year by then. I kept on getting these complaints from the Navajo people about the activities of traders and their questionable practices in trading and pricing of goods.

Iverson: Like pawn, for example?

Zah: Yes. It was one of those situations where the Navajo people would come in seeking legal assistance from the advocates or from the lawyers, on many occasions, by stating that the traders are acting like pawnbrokers. They're the bankers. They are like the post office for local people where they can pick up their letters, open it, and see what's inside. And then they were also lending out money at unbelievable interest rates to their favorite community members. They were also acting as an employment agency for the railroad companies. I believe they had contracts with the railroad and the United States Postal Service to provide those services to the local people; however, they abused the system.

One complaint that I was getting from many of the Navajo people was about the pawn system. They would say, "I pawned my saddle, my jewelry, I pawned the very precious possession I had at the trading post. A month or two later I would go back and would find they had the prices jacked up too high, and that's not what I pawned the article for."

Traders did not give pawn tickets or receipts. There was nothing that would show the interest rate and the appropriate value of the pawned article. Another complaint I was getting was a complete lack of notice from the traders to inform the customers about receiving their Social Security check or checks from the Navajo Nation government, or the railroad for unemployment compensation. The people complained that they didn't know when the trader had received the check. It might have been two or three weeks before they came to the trading post, and it wasn't until they ran up a bill for about $100 that had to be cleared. The trader would then say, "Hey, you have run up a bill for $100 that needs to be cleared. I have a check here for you for $120. You have $20 left. I want you to sign the check over to me." Naturally, the local people were very upset about this kind of business.

Taking on the Traders

An independent legal services program without many resources can only do and handle those kinds of cases on a very limited basis, because we didn't have the information we needed at our disposal. Our clients who spoke limited English did not have the necessary information. So there was really no law or regulation that governed activities between customers and the merchant either by the tribe or by the federal government.

Therefore, in the summer of 1969, I talked with some Navajo college students. They were very conscientious students who cared about the Navajo people. One of those nine students is now a member of the Navajo Supreme Court. Another student is a superintendent of a well-known school in Arizona. These students were very aggressive; they were also very smart. They knew exactly what they wanted to do, and so we sat and we talked. We had a long, long discussion about what we should do, because DNA could only do so much. They wanted to be involved. We then decided to organize a non-profit group and called it Southwest Indian Development. It was commonly known among the students as SID.

SID was a non-profit corporate entity. The students raised their own funds to do action research on trading post operations. United Scholarship Service, Inc., from Denver, Colorado, agreed to pay stipends for the nine students to do what they called "action research." That research was a classic example of how research should be done.

Nowadays, I go to conferences where students do research from colleges and universities on Indian land. In many cases, they are just doing research maybe for the sake of doing research. They don't really have a full-blown purpose for why they are doing research. And the research on the trading posts was designed to cause some movement or action by the tribe or federal government to do something about the terrible abuse the traders were causing the local people. I was the executive director of SID, and I was also the deputy director of DNA People's Legal Services. SID was a side job for me—a non-paid position. A lot of young volunteers supported the SID program. This same group got involved in demonstrating

against the Gallup Intertribal Indian Ceremonial during the summer of 1969 to raise consciousness about the exploitation and greed of the ceremonial event.

Conducting Surveys

The students said, "We want to participate in a meaningful way. What we want to do is to go out to the trading post and begin asking some questions. We know that a lot of these commodities they're selling have a tremendous markup. We want to do the survey on their pricing system." For example, coffee, potatoes, canned food, your basic staples. They compared those prices with prices in Gallup, New Mexico, and Farmington, New Mexico. They saw how these markup prices were outrageous—anywhere from 30 to 120 percent markup.

The students also wanted to survey prices for meat, bacon, pork chops, and mutton. They found that in some cases, some of the traders were selling spoiled meat because the refrigeration wasn't all that good. They saw where some food sold was unsanitary. The traders would say to those customers, "Make sure that you cook it very well." The students actually heard or overheard some of those instructions. They recorded that information and included it as part of their research and a report they produced.

The students really got annoyed and angry over some of their findings. They decided to publish the report for the full Navajo Council and to present it specifically to the Navajo trading post committee. But this committee did not offer any help or even read the report and try to do something about the horrible situation. They looked at these young people and said these are just young, radical, college-educated kids that were looking for something to do during the summer. The Navajo leadership really didn't listen to them.

And then they went over to the Bureau of Indian Affairs [BIA]. Graham Holmes was the area director. They had a session with him. I remember Graham Holmes saying, "I live here in Window Rock and sometimes I go to chapter meetings and meet with people every day. I have never heard Navajo people complaining about the

traders." So he brushed that aside. He told the students that they didn't have any basis to make these kinds of charges and complaints.

The students wanted him to do something. The traders were federally licensed by his office. They were licensed on the Navajo reservation to do business among the Navajo people. At that time, there was something like one hundred trading posts throughout the Navajo Nation. The students wanted the BIA area director to promulgate rules and regulations to govern commerce activities so that it was fair to everyone.

The Federal Trade Commission

However, Graham Holmes didn't want to protect the Navajo people from the unfair practices. The students didn't get discouraged, but instead said, "Hey, we have a situation where the Navajo Nation and the BIA don't want to do anything. The Tribal Court proceedings take a long time, and it becomes expensive. So what do we do now?" they asked. And that's when they decided that they should approach the Federal Trade Commission in Washington, D.C. They approached the Federal Trade Commission and asked it to come out to the Navajo Nation for a hearing and review some of the studies and the research that the students put together on trading post activities.

The Federal Trade Commission held a hearing in Window Rock, where they subpoenaed the area director and some tribal officials. Members of the commission were just outraged about the markup of prices and some questionable activities. They were shocked that there were not rules and regulations to govern the traders' prices and practices. They collected all of the testimony and documents and used them to force the BIA to develop some mechanism to remedy the unfair business practices. As a result, the United States Department of the Interior finally promulgated rules and regulations that governed the activities of the traders and their relationships with Navajo customers.

The regulations clearly stated that when a Navajo person comes to a trading post to pawn whatever property, the trader is obligated by the new regulation to provide a pawn ticket showing the interest

rate per month and year. The traders can't sell those pawned items as long as the customer is paying interest. Prior to these regulations, some traders were selling pawned items to visitors and tourists. Indian jewelry and artifacts were in high demand by tourists on any reservation. There was nothing that would prohibit the trader from selling the items at a high price. The new rules and regulations took care of that by giving customers a pawn ticket.

Iverson: In *Navajo Trading: The End of an Era*, Willow Roberts Powers blamed "radical" DNA attorneys such as Bob Hilgendorf and John Silko for their harsh criticism of trader practices. She argued these DNA employees sought not regulation but annihilation and claimed they expedited the departure of many traders. DNA may have served as a convenient scapegoat for defenders of the trading posts, but other factors figured more fully in the traders' continuing decline. Navajo roads had been improved, and far more Navajos had access to cars and trucks. Increased proficiency in English and greater familiarity with the larger American society also made a difference. In addition, a lower percentage of the people raised livestock and wove rugs.

Zah: And so the traders then rebelled by saying, "We can't do business here anymore—there's too much paperwork for us to do." They said that they couldn't continue to do business under these circumstances. Some of the traders decided then to close their stores. They were upset that the federal government, with the blessing of the tribal government, would have these rules and regulations enacted.

This is quite a success story. By just having young people of nine students come together, and they said, "We're going to focus on this, and we're going to try to do something about it. In the end we wanted to have fair treatment from the traders in their dealings with the Navajo people."

It didn't take one summer. It took two years to do this, but they kept at it. The following summer, almost all the same students came back, just to do follow-up work on their research project. I take a lot of pride in those young people doing what they did. No student should ever say we can't really do much about these things. Here's a situation where nine students, banding together, found the resources in order to solve a huge problem. And at the end, all

they were looking for was decent and fair treatment of local Navajo customers, and to have access to sanitary food. They also wanted to have an audience with Navajo leadership so they could be heard about this problem.

Iverson: Can you tell me a little more about some of these students?

Zah: Well, I remember one of the students was Gloria Hale-Showalter, who graduated from Window Rock High School and went to Fort Lewis College. She got her master's degree and became superintendent of Window Rock and Sanders High School for several years. She is a highly respected young lady, very smart, and successful in her own right. She was an individual who really cared about the Navajo people.

Another student was Lorene Bennett Ferguson, who also went to Fort Lewis and on to the University of New Mexico Law School where she received her law degree and ultimately became an associate justice on the Navajo Nation Supreme Court. Judge Ferguson is such a dedicated person to Navajo people and always supportive of the young people.

Michael Benson is another student who is just an outstanding individual. He is now working with the Department of Water Resources on Navajo water rights issues.

I was just blessed with having these kinds of people come forth, and they were volunteering their services to the project. They knew that this wasn't going to be easy because it meant changing people's attitude and challenging them and pressuring the members of the Navajo Council. Also they tried to persuade the Federal Trade Commission [FTC] to come out and have a hearing using some of the research materials that they collected. They wanted the FTC to force the BIA to come up with some type of rules and regulations.

Railroad Labor

Railroad work away from the reservation was an important source of income for local labor. By entering into some kind of agreement, the traders were able to select local community members who would go

on the railroad job. And railroad work is hard work, and so they were looking for middle-age and some young people to go on these jobs.

The railroad industry entered into these agreements with the local traders. It took advantage of that by looking for some young men who owed them money on their credits.

They looked for those kinds of people. And when they found those individuals, they would encourage the individuals to do business at their store. The customers would run up credits. Then they would ask individuals, "We can sell you these items, and we'll just charge it against your name." When there were enough charges to the local person, he would say, "Hey, I got this railroad job, and we want to recommend that you go to work next week. If you want to work, be here at eight o'clock in the morning—we'll drive you to Holbrook, Arizona, and then we'll put you on the train to your work station somewhere in the United States. And you're going to be working there for eight months to a year or so."

When the traders did that, they were able to provide the railroad companies what they wanted—cheap labor. If there were any checks coming from their work, they were able to intercept those at the trading post, and that's how the traders controlled that poor individual.

Zah: I remember back when the BIA commissioner, and later the assistant secretary of Indian Affairs, would come out to a conference. We would ask them to respond to our lawsuit. And we would explain that they had a responsibility over the trading post operations. The traders on the Navajo Nation were out there because you gave them a license and lease for $25 a year.

The federal officials may not have wanted to regulate the traders, but we kept after them. If they came close to the Navajo reservation, they knew that we were going to be there to ask them questions about their lack of action about the trading posts.

In the meantime, the Navajo Nation started building shopping centers throughout the reservation in strategic places. By having a shopping center and having grocery stores, the Navajo people got better prices for the food and goods they were getting. Admittedly they may have had to drive some distances, but they always had done business in local areas. The shopping centers really replaced the function of the trading posts.

The federal postal services then began going out into communities like Pinon. They established a post office, with individual boxes and numbers. The Navajo people then could come to the post office and pick up their mail. They didn't have to deal with the traders.

To me it was not a good idea for the traders to have this powerful role in the community. But at the same time, the students, myself and others, knew that it just had to change. And the transition between shopping centers, building post offices at these local communities was a big transition.

6

Neighbors

"Much of What We Faced with the Hopi Nation Was Something Created by the Federal Government"

IN 1882, PRESIDENT CHESTER ALAN ARTHUR signed an executive order that divided a three-and-one-half-million-acre parcel in northern Arizona between the Navajos and Hopis. Through this action, the land was reserved "for the use and occupancy of the Moqui and such other Indians as the Secretary may see fit to settle thereon." The Navajos pushed westward during the latter half of the nineteenth century. Many Navajos escaped the Long Walk to Fort Sumner by hiding out in areas such as Black Mesa, Navajo Mountain, and other remote Western locales. Navajo economic growth following the Navajo Treaty of 1868 was boosted by the expansion. At the same time, some Hopis pushed eastward, taking over many fields that had been abandoned by Navajos forced from the area.

In the period following the Navajo Treaty of 1868, the Navajos continued to occupy more land and attempted to gain control over that territory. Much of the land that the Navajos occupied was outside those initial boundaries. This continuing effort to extend the boundaries led perhaps inevitably to conflict with the Hopi people. The value of this acreage increased over time, in part due to the coal and other mineral resources found within this area.

The Executive Order of 1882 practically guaranteed trouble. The vague wording of the order did not state precisely which acres would

be used by the Navajos and which by the Hopis. In addition, non-Indian ranchers, farmers, and other businessmen sought to reduce Navajo livestock grazing. Indian Agent J. H. Fleming, stationed at Keams Canyon, had no interest in long-term federal service. As soon as President Arthur signed off on the order Fleming had crafted, the agent signed off too. He resigned his post and moved to California, never to return. The Navajos and the Hopis remained.

There would have been problems with honoring any agreement. Two developments exacerbated the situation. One concerned the status of the livestock industry, and the other focused on the use of natural resources. The livestock reduction program of the 1930s and 1940s had finally been abandoned, but the ill-advised policy had devastated an already uncertain business. For the Navajos who raised livestock, the livestock reduction program imposed on the Navajos and the Hopis proved devastating. As time went on, an increasing percentage of the Navajos began to search for other options.

During the 1930s, the government divided Navajo and Hopi lands into eighteen land management districts, with the Hopis occupying District 6 for administrative purposes. The government imposed restrictions on the number of sheep and other livestock each family could raise. As their economic situation deteriorated and as more people were forced to move away from their land and homes, people became separated from their familiar surroundings. Years later an old Navajo woman remembered what had been lost: "It nearly killed me to move even a short distance. I prefer the old place although we lived poorly. We had space, privacy, and livestock. We had everything."

Many Navajos and Hopis had known for many years about the economic potential of the coal at Black Mesa. They also were concerned about the impact of coal mining on the land and the water that would be used to slurry the coal over two hundred miles to its eventual destination, Clark County, Nevada.

The Navajos had long hoped they could use the courts to improve their position in regard to land used, but in *Healing v. Jones*, the United States District Court, District of Arizona, ruled the Hopis held "joint, undivided, and equal rights and interests within the 1882 reservation." They also maintained sole use of Land Management District 6 within these lands.

The election of Ivan Sidney as Hopi president signaled the two nations might be able to negotiate more constructively than they had in the past. However, the economic stakes were too high and animosity too deeply rooted for meaningful results to be realized. Peter MacDonald's sharp criticism of Zah on this matter helped him regain the chairmanship of the Navajo Tribal Council in 1986.

Ivan Sidney

Zah: Hopi leader Ivan Sidney went to Phoenix Indian School. He was in back of me maybe a couple years, maybe even three years. And I got to know him some back then. And then subsequent to both of us leaving Phoenix Indian School, our paths crossed here and there periodically, with him as a police officer, and then me working at DNA People's Legal Services. I was contacted by Navajo people who were incarcerated in Hopi courts, and by the Hopi police, and because of the work that DNA must do in protecting our clients'

Hopi leader and longtime friend Ivan Sidney (middle) appears with Peterson Zah (right) and Harry Kinney, mayor of Albuquerque, (left) at a special event honoring the work of Sidney and Zah.

rights and all of that. We were able to see each other every once in a while. I liked him; I always did. I liked his demeanor and his openness to things, suggestions, and all of that. As a result of my being acquainted with him, I got to know his family. His wife was a very cordial, pleasant individual, and Ivan was very dedicated to the Hopi people, Hopi culture, and she was also dedicated to the work that Ivan was doing. I got to know them fairly well even prior to the election.

When I came to ASU, their daughter went to school at ASU West. I had some conversations with her, and on some occasions counseled with her, and she approached me seeking some explanation on the issues, and maybe even seeking help from the university. I also know his boys and other children that he was very close to, and maybe the children of his own relatives. He was one of those individuals that was very important in my life.

Announcement from Low Mountain

When I prepared to run for the Navajo Nation chairman, he came to my announcement at Low Mountain in January of 1982. I remember that day. It had snowed the night before, and we were kind of concerned about the snow and the mud, and all of that, and the cold air coming in from the north. It looked like it was going to bring in some more snow, and we were concerned about the people coming to Low Mountain. We thought there might not be many people coming. We were surprised. I was completely taken aback by over one thousand people showing up at that opening announcement.

Ivan Sidney and some of the council delegates from the Hopi Nation were in the crowd. They were there to observe and to get acquainted with people. People came from Polacca. Polacca and Low Mountain are maybe some ten, twelve miles apart. Many of the Hopi people had gone to the Keams Canyon store and trading post. Many of them also went to the Keams Canyon Boarding School, as did many local Navajos. So they knew each other from the past— going to school together and meeting each other at the trading post. Ivan Sidney knew some Navajo families, and some Navajo people

knew him. So it was just natural that he came to my announcement back in 1982.

I guess some political advisors thought it was all constructed to have a major political impact, because at that time the Hopi Nation was having difficulty getting the attention of the Navajo people. Some people thought that it was all orchestrated for political reasons. But what they didn't know was that it was just a natural thing for that to happen, because they were neighbors. If a major event was taking place in your community, you go visit, greet, and you converse with your neighbors. That's basically what happened. Our relationship has been very cordial right from the beginning. Of course, people know that we invited him to my inauguration and he was there at the inauguration ceremony, participating in all of the events and ceremonies.

Transitions

When I look at the Hopi situation today in 2010, and over the past two or three years especially, I believe that most Indian peoples are going through what the Hopis are going through. Many of the Hopi people still believe in the traditional old ways, and they want to maintain some of those qualities that tradition brings. Then there are other people who are more progressive, modern in their outlook on life, politics.

If you put those two together, the old and the new, the traditional and the new, you will always have some degree of contention, and there will be some spirited discussion that takes place between the two parties. That's no different than anywhere else. Even in the United States, we are experiencing that right now. Some people believe in certain political persuasions or situations, and others disagree. Democracy and our country promote that.

Among the Indian people, in Indian country you know, the modern concepts come from the school experience, and you have the traditionalists continuing to live in the traditional way. Neither is bad. I think people just need to understand it. The Hopi people are having that discussion right now among their community members and

Inauguration ceremonies for Peterson Zah as chairman of the Navajo
Tribal Council.

their villages. They have their own government at the local village level, and they also have a centralized government. They are trying to make things work so that the government is responsive to the wishes of, perhaps, maybe the villages and some of the local people.

That's going to take time, to understand clearly what that all means to the future of the Hopi Nation. Personally, I just wish them well, and then hope for the best, because they are just like any American Indian tribe. This is a small group with a small government. They are going through those trying times right now. The Navajos, on the other hand, were also going through the same process. There are a lot of questions about the way the Navajo government is set up. There are a lot of questions about the illegal activities of tribal government officials, and how their constituents are not agreeing with, perhaps, some of the demands that they put on their tribal council delegate. That kind of a discussion is taking place. It's really about accountability, where they like to see the council delegates being accountable for anything they do. We are having the same kind of problem. In the state of Arizona here in the Southwest, you have Apaches who are going through the same process. It's basically almost the same issue. They are having economic hard times right now in 2010. It just puts a lot of stress on the tribal government, and I think a lot of the Indian people are feeling that. And it certainly has filtered down to the Hopis, Navajos, Apaches, and other tribes.

Much of what we faced with the Hopi Nation was something that was created by the federal government. It was basically something that the federal government decided that it should resolve these issues in certain ways. Unfortunately, many of our people didn't really think of it that way. They just had us fighting each other for years and years.

A Complicated Matter

The Navajo–Hopi land dispute is very complicated. It went through so many generations of Navajo and Hopi people, and many leadership changes as well. When I went into the chairmanship in 1983, I believed in the concept that the Hopi people aren't going anywhere and the Navajos aren't going anywhere either. We might as well get along with one another and begin getting acquainted with each

Peterson Zah (left) and Louis Denetsosie (right) point to a map related to the ongoing struggle for land use between the Navajos and the Hopis.

other—regardless of what the land dispute brought to the people. We have to coexist, and we have to live in a peaceful way. That was my philosophy going into my chairmanship. I would make every effort to befriend the Hopi Nation. Only through friendship and through understanding what we were made of could we bring about understanding and love for each other and between our people.

Because of what we thought about one another at the time, the Hopi young people and the Navajo young people were intermarrying. So that meant that we as leaders had to look at those kinds of statistics among the young people.

I thought that with my election and Ivan Sidney's election we had a perfect opportunity to bring the two tribes back together. But it was very difficult for both of us, because on both sides of the issue were people who were not really accepting what we were trying to do. We knew that in the long run, if we could give it a try, and if we could begin to put people back on the right track of a friendly coexistence, that in the long run it would work out.

We knew that it was a big, heavy political risk, on both sides, for us to do that. But my friend Ivan Sidney was tenacious, and he just

had the right attitude. He had a lot of courage to do what he did. We then began the long, long road to healing. Something like thirty years have passed, and we still have a lot of work to do. What really makes me happy is to see the progress that's taking place. The two tribes are beginning to work together.

In the different agreements that we now have, we recognize each other as sovereign nations. There are some problems that exist between the two, but we have agreed to disagree. That's different than the way the Navajo Nation and the Hopi Nation were going after each other, way back in the early 1970s, and even further back into the 1960s.

Changing the Dispute

We changed the whole complexion of the Navajo–Hopi land dispute. Here I am thirty years later—I'm just glad that we did what we did, because it just had to be done. There were just too many resources being spent from both sides to fight one another. It was better to come together where we have to disagree with respect and dignity, knowing that in the long run, the goal is to have the two tribes come together and become friends like they have been in the past.

Here are two examples of cooperation between the Hopis and the Navajos. The uranium tailings had to be dealt with in the Tuba City area. When the wind came in early spring, it blew the uranium tailings everywhere on Navajo land as well as on Hopi land. It landed on our animals, on the grass, on the people. The uranium tailings did not discriminate between Navajo and Hopi. They landed where they may. And as a result, the doctors at Indian Health Service had to take care of many, many patients that were getting cancer to their bodies. No one really knows how much of that came from the uranium tailing dust that was blowing all over the place.

So Ivan Sidney and I had to agree, from the Navajo and from the Hopi side, to cooperate and bring the federal government out there so that the process of remediating the uranium tailings could begin. And as a result, within something like three or four years, they were able to pay for the cost of remediation and covering the uranium tailings so that it's not dangerous. They had to make it so

Members of the Hopi Nation also raised sheep, which competed with the sheep on the Navajo Nation for grazing land. These sheep belonged to the Taylors, a prominent Hopi family.

Hopis also became enthusiastic participants in basketball. This game took place at the Shungopavi Day School in 1944.

that it's safe for a thousand years. That could only be done if you had a commitment from both tribes. We needed permission from the Hopis and the Hopis needed permission from the Navajos to present a resolution to the federal government. That was the only way that the federal government could fund the project.

The roads provide a second example. We needed more all-weather roads. Many of our tribal members had to drive pickup trucks through sand and gravel and through mud. We didn't enjoy all kinds of miles and miles of all-weather road. So we created what we called a Turquoise Trail that would begin from the Hopi Nation's land and go into Navajo. It would be a federally funded program. Because of the rain and snow of winter and spring, we really needed more all-weather roads. Through intertribal agreement between the two nations, we were able to support this plan. The late senator Barry Goldwater really pushed the plan through Congress to get it appropriated. Unfortunately, when we left office, the leaders after us really did not pick up the slack. It never got finished to our satisfaction.

Hopi High School is another good example. The Hopis needed Navajo support to build those facilities, and Ivan Sidney and I worked together to do that. We had children from the Navajo side as well as children from the Hopi side that needed education. They were shutting down the boarding schools here in Phoenix and in California and Oklahoma and Nevada. So we needed a local public school where Navajo and Hopi kids could go. And as a result, the federal government created Hopi High School. That was only possible through cooperation between the two tribes. You need cooperation for the tribes to make any kind of meaningful progress that will benefit the young generations of the Navajo and Hopi people.

The land dispute is a very complicated issue. It's been going on for over a hundred years. So it was not easy to deal with. But I was very fortunate to have leadership from the Hopi Nation that was able to buy into some of the things that we were both promoting. So I can't say that I'm completely responsible for it—it's something that the Hopi Nation and its leaders also had to push, as well as other people that I was working with.

There are two main arguments that I have heard. Many of the people in this area were among the more traditional and more separate members of the two nations. Relocation became particularly

The Navajos and the Hopis claimed certain areas of land, including areas like Black Mesa, the land formation seen in the distance from Canyon de Chelly.

difficult for them because you could never, obviously, provide an exactly identical kind of environment. And if you moved into Pinon some of the people in Pinon had mixed emotions about it. But since the number of people living in the traditional way declined, the disputes over grazing and other matters were reduced because a smaller percentage of the people were living in the old way.

But I've also heard it argued, on the other hand, that this decline made it more difficult for the people to continue with the old way. Many of them were elderly. They were particularly unhappy to move to a new location or to change from the old ways.

They didn't really have any choice except to seek some other alternative, which was to move in with their children. In some cases, those children were removed already from the Navajo and Hopi land. It's something that made the relocation program very complicated, and it was such an emotional issue for many, many families.

Being Uprooted

Federal officials thought all we had to do was to make some houses available for Navajo people who wanted to move off the Navajo reservation and into nearby cities and towns. They believed that's all we had to do to resolve the issue. But it didn't work out that way because so many Navajo people lived a certain lifestyle. They wanted to continue to live on the same land and wanted to continue to graze livestock. When you uproot people from those kinds of situations all of a sudden in one year, for example, and put them into an urban setting where they have to pay taxes on their homes, when they have to do all these other things that they weren't accustomed to, then it became a difficult issue.

It's extremely difficult for those particular families to live that kind of a lifestyle and begin changing all of a sudden within a matter of six months to a year—to completely change their attitudes, their lifestyle, to the lifestyle of the urban people. The changes were unacceptable to many of the Navajo people who moved. And that's why it became such an emotional issue.

So the relocation program never really succeeded. In the late 1940s and early 1950s, the federal government had this massive relocation program. And the whole idea was to get the Indian people off their reservations, put them into urban areas, and let them become gainfully employed, and let them buy homes. They would have their children here, and they would become urbanized, and they would be just like any of us taxpaying citizens. And that was the plan. The whole situation turned out to be more complicated and difficult than many people expected.

7

Resources

"There Are Tremendous
Opportunities Out There"

MANY NON-INDIAN AMERICANS SAW economic development on Indian reservations as something that could not or should not occur. Some saw American Indian communities as inherently unable to gain equal status in American society. Portraying Indians as victims rather than as victors reflected a negative view of indigenous communities. Indian reservations were seen as ghettos rather than homelands, and the Indian story tended to be told as tragedy rather than as triumph.

Yet it became clear in the 1970s that the Navajo Nation was committed to finding ways to use its resources more fully and effectively. But industrial development had never been greeted by universal applause within the Navajo Nation. During the era before World War II, Navajo leaders Chee Dodge and Jacob Morgan quarreled about where any proceeds from a mineral lease should be directed. Dodge argued for giving top priority to the Navajo Nation in general, while Morgan favored returning more money to the local communities more impacted by this kind of development.

In an area where few people had gained experience in running a business, tribal enterprises seemed to furnish the possibility of obtaining more extensive returns from land resources. For a number

The Navajo Forest Products Industry plant employed many Navajo workers.

of years, for example, the Navajo Forest Products Industry (NFPI) enjoyed sustained economic growth. Retired business executives from outside companies worked with Navajo employees to take advantage of Navajo timber. Eventually, the workings of the international timber industry unraveled, and NFPI had to close its doors. The ultimate hope, Zah often stated, rested in the promise of different generations from within the Navajo Nation working together to develop Navajo resources in a productive and responsible manner.

To be sure, one can define words like productive and responsible in different ways. Some forms of "development" could be more contested, given past experience and local sensitivities. Ninety-nine-year leases were often employed in the 1950s to gain what amounted to a sale when an actual sale could not occur. As time went on, Indians generally gained a more informed sense of what was at stake.

Navajo employees sort lumber at the Navajo Forest Products Industry facility.

Tourism offered another form of economic development. Visitors to Navajo country often held romantic views of Indian peoples. Although individual Navajos gained employment in this sector, they did not begin to prosper as did owners or operators of tourist facilities including motels, campgrounds, parks, and other components, which yielded profits to outside interests and local traders. However, after the end of World War II, the Navajo Nation moved decisively to gain a larger percentage of this substantial market. In the 1940s and 1950s, the Arts and Crafts Guild enjoyed some success in encouraging tourist purchases of Navajo weaving, silversmithing, and other arts. Individual Navajos also began forging partnerships with non-Navajo partners to build and operate hotels, motels, and other tourist-related businesses. Richard Mike became one of the best-known Navajo entrepreneurs, gaining strategically situated

Jeeps move tourists through Canyon de Chelly. Canyon de Chelly was a major draw for tourists.

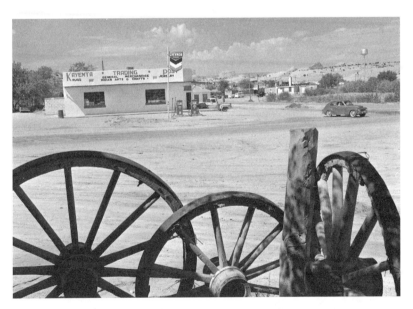

Kayenta begins to confront the age of modern tourism. About twenty-five miles south of Monument Valley, Kayenta benefited from its proximity to that destination.

Burger King franchises, among other examples of indigenous entrepreneurialism.

During the late 1960s and 1970s, romantic attitudes about seemingly almost all things Indian brought in revenue, but also encouraged an avalanche of junk. When the newly elected MacDonald administration decided in 1972 to transform the Arts and Crafts Guild into the Navajo Arts and Crafts Enterprise, it wound up creating a mechanism for the mediocre. Brought in to turn around an operation that had lost a million dollars in five years, Raymond Smith salvaged a rapidly sinking ship. He had run a grocery store and served in the Marines and on the Navajo Tribal Council. Although retired, he could not resist what he termed "a great challenge." Smith turned around the enterprise and led it successfully for more than twenty years.[1]

Of course, tourism today is linked to casinos, and the Indian nations of the Southwest have rarely been reticent in their efforts to take advantage of this relatively new form of economic development. The size of the Navajo Nation and the size of the Navajo population, however, raised questions that do not always emerge in smaller communities. A smaller Indian nation may be tempted to funnel some of its profits into per capita payments or be pushed to find some way of furnishing funds for tribal members who live a good distance away from their home country rather than investing in the common good: diabetes, children, the elderly, and so forth. To date, per capita has been less attractive at Navajo given its large population.

Another potential dilemma may surface in regard to how a community may see itself. Prior to casinos, most Southwestern Indian nations were not prosperous. Today, the elders at the Fort McDowell Yavapai Nation recall all too well the tremendous poverty that gripped the reservation. Leaders such as Clinton Pattea worry that the young have only known prosperity. How will they respond to adversity?

Certainly there is evidence in Navajo communities and elsewhere of a willingness to reexamine past policies and priorities. Within the Navajo Nation, the closing of the Black Mesa coal mine has surely signaled changing times. Even though the mining operation did

Monument Valley at sunrise. The Navajo Nation has recently opened The View Hotel at this site.

provide some employment in an area where good jobs remained very hard to find, more than a few Navajos seemed glad to see Peabody Coal Company close its doors. They saw promise in developing solar- and wind-energy resources. As one member of the Nation put it, "Solar would be long-term. Solar and wind: we don't have a problem with that. It's pretty windy out here."[2]

Casino development at Navajo has been more gradual than in most other locations for a number of reasons, as Zah explains in this chapter. The initial Navajo ventures into gaming have done very well, indeed. The biggest success to date has been the Navajos' Fire Rock Navajo Casino, just outside of Gallup.

According to Navajo officials, Fire Rock is the first example of an Indian nation using its own money to build a casino instead of

going to outside sources for funding. Since its opening in November 2008, Fire Rock has been a huge success. Perhaps the most interesting dimension to this new enterprise may be the customer base for the casino. Ninety-five percent of these folks have at least one thing in common. They are members of the same Indian nation: the Navajo Nation.

The Navajos are taking Ned Hatathli's words to heart. They are becoming more future oriented. Zah's initiatives while serving as chairman or president in regard to establishing various trust funds reveals him as someone not only committed to dealing with contemporary concerns but also looking toward tomorrow and the needs and concerns of different sectors of the Navajo Nation. The very existence of the trust funds offered another instance where he tried to deal with both contemporary concerns and the long-term needs of an increasingly complex community.

Taxing Companies

Zah: In the mid-1980s, the taxing of major companies doing business on the reservation began to be seriously considered. These included companies who wanted to develop oil, gas, coal, and other minerals, as well as the expansion of transportation, and convenience stores. These companies challenged the authority of the Navajo Nation to collect the business activity tax (BAT) and possessory interest tax (PIT) which was passed by the council in 1978. The Navajo Tax Commission indicated that these were businesses that were willing taxpayers, but some were protesting and refusing to pay. That led to the filing of the lawsuit *Kerr-McGee Corp. v. Navajo Tribe of Indians.*

We called a meeting of the groups to try to see if we could come up with some kind of an understanding or solution or at least agree to disagree if need be. Kerr-McGee Corporation, a mining company, joined by other business entities, became a major plaintiff. And one of the things that they were saying was that "we question the authority that you are using to tax us." Those corporate representatives were saying, "We question the authority that you are using to

tax us. That particular resolution is not supported by the secretary of the interior and this is an illegal resolution." One of them indicated that they had a business contract that had been signed by the Navajo Nation as a government. Those contracts were signed by the chairman, the council, and finally by representatives from the Bureau of Indian Affairs and the Department of the Interior. These were legitimate legal documents. The companies did not want to pay taxes.

I thanked the group for coming and being honest about their position that they would go all the way to the U.S. Supreme Court. They believed they could get a favorable ruling. Some agreed to pay into an escrow account pending the final decision by the courts.

Annie Wauneka was there along with a couple of elderly Navajo council delegates. They pleaded with the companies by saying everywhere else you go, you have to pay taxes. For example, Peabody Coal Company was doing business in West Virginia and Utah, and it had to pay taxes to the states.

The Navajo Council delegates argued that the Navajo Nation is a government just like the states, and they wanted the Navajo Nation to be treated the same as these states by business entities. The Supreme Court agreed and came down with a decision on April 14, 1985. On that date we got a notice from the U.S. Supreme Court that we had won the case. The vote among the justices was nine to zero. This short decision reinforced the legitimacy of the Navajo Nation government with a duly elected Navajo Tribal Council elected by the local people. Non-Navajo corporations should not question the legitimacy of the Navajo government, the most elaborate government of all the Indian tribes in the United States.

The deposit in the escrow account was now about $217 million. This was extra money separate and apart from the regular annual tribal revenue, money that was undesignated and not yet earmarked for any program. I went out into the communities and started listening to people as to what we should do with the surplus funds. The local people started saying that when the Tribal Council came into session, all they did was spend, spend, spend. It was high time, they said, that we began saving money for our children and secure their future and the future of the Navajo Nation.

Developing Trust Funds

That's when the concept of developing trust funds came into discussion. However, the need in the community was so great that in some chapters it overshadowed the dialogue. We then decided to take a hard look at some of the existing programs like the Navajo tribal scholarship program for students. We heard reports that they only had something like eight or nine million dollars left, but that over ten thousand students applied for those funds each year. It was then decided to put twenty million dollars into the scholarship trust fund so that the interest earned each year, plus whatever amount the BIA could contribute, could be used to support the education of our youth at various colleges and universities throughout the country.

There were also several funds created from donations from individual corporations, foundations that supplemented the scholarship program. Using those funds, the Navajo Nation has aided approximately ten thousand students each year.

The other fund that was created back then was called the Nation Building Fund. We had 110 chapter houses that always needed funds to operate the local government. Actually, they were helping build a nation without much financial help on a systematic basis from the central Navajo government. The Nation Building Fund was also created with a sixty-million-dollar trust fund. They would share the interest each year, and the local people could decide on the use of the funds.

There were something like six or seven trust funds started to take care of some of the most pressing issues facing the Navajo people. Funds were set aside for the elderly, handicapped, college preparatory schools, and vocational education.

The Land Acquisition Fund

In my second term as president we also established the Land Acquisition Fund. A small percentage of the total tribal revenues was set aside each year to support this program. The idea here was to build

a significant amount within fifteen to twenty years so that the tribe could purchase those lands that are placed on the market, especially land that is adjacent to the Navajo Nation.

The whole idea was that we needed to enlarge the Navajo Nation, because we had a young population that's growing faster than the national average. They demanded more space and elbow room. Some wanted to become livestock owners and go into ranching for a living. That's why we established the Land Acquisition Fund.

The Land Acquisition Fund did very well and grew to fifty-three million dollars in 2008, and the Resources Committee has oversight and responsibility over this fund. The committee recently entered into a business agreement with the Navajo Nation Gaming Enterprise to use about thirty-five million dollars to build the first Navajo casino in Gallup, New Mexico. This casino made money and employed hundreds of people. The interest generated by the casino should yield greater profits to the Land Acquisition Fund.

The Permanent Trust Fund

The Permanent Trust Fund began during my administration. We started it with a deposit of $26 million. The Permanent Fund grew beyond anybody's imagination. The money managers, the lawyers who put this resolution together, and the Navajo leadership were surprised that it did better than expected. At the height of its growth, it was leveling off at $1.4 billion.

The Permanent Fund took a big hit in 2008/2009 and went down to about $880 million, but then worked its way back up again as our economy slowly recovered. The tribal government should leave the principal alone and allow it to grow again. They should also not spend the interest earned in foolish ways without the people's input and consent. The Permanent Fund is the people's saving account, and sometimes it's the only thing we have. The council should not put their sticky hands into the fund without the people's permission.

We are one of the few tribes that have assets and trust funds that are not designated beyond our means and income. There are gaming

tribes that generate a lot of revenue, but they also have to pay bills. They have put themselves in huge debt by building those facilities and doing large-scale economic development programs.

At some point in the history of the Navajo people, we have had to come together to decide how those monies should be used by referendum vote as indicated in the Permanent Fund.

The Per Capita Issue

Iverson: To divide it on a per capita basis?

Zah: Some have suggested that. I receive e-mails, telephone calls, and letters when I go back. People always talk to me about it. There are some groups that want to start spending that money. For example, the 2008 judiciary committee of the Navajo Council had a resolution or bill to take $153 million out of the Permanent Fund to build five to seven jails. They said, "Holding facilities where we can incarcerate the lawless and the alcoholics." Nothing was ever said about rehabilitating the people. I went back to the Navajo Council and lobbied against that. Fortunately, the full council voted it down and defeated the concept. I was encouraged by some of the delegates to hold onto this money, to keep it in trust for the young people for the future of the Navajo Nation.

The young people should do a lot of the things that the Navajo people need. There are tremendous opportunities out there. If young people can get a decent education and develop skills, they can cause a major impact throughout the Navajo Nation. That is something that I continuously advocate to the young people.

That's what we need to begin doing now. By law, before any expenditure occurs on the principal of the Permanent Fund, there has to be a referendum vote by the local people. In other words, the council can't just come in and say, "We want to use $153 million," pass a resolution by majority, and then begin using those monies. They can't do it that way.

The tribal law says when they are going into spending the principal, they have to inform the people and conduct a referendum vote on exactly how some of those funds are used. The use and

expenditure of the interest earned are different in that it only takes a council resolution. You have to have a two-thirds vote of the council and probably some participation on the part of the local people, in terms of them having an input on what is being talked about.

That's what the Permanent Fund and your trust fund are all about. At some point, all of the Navajo people, the voters, have to come together, and we have to have a sense of direction. Where are the Navajo people going right now? In what direction should we all be headed? Not until you decide those kinds of directions can you faithfully say that this is the way we want to begin spending the Navajo Nation trust fund. There has to be a sense of direction before we can start putting a program together as to how this one should be done.

An issue that's going to be prevalent in the next several years is Navajo off-reservation residence and employment. Take a look at the Navajo population of over three hundred thousand people. How many of them live on the reservation, and how many live off the reservation? We're about split in half right now. There always has been a majority of the Navajo people living on the reservation. But because of education and jobs, many of the Navajos have migrated into Phoenix. In my own family, I never thought that this would happen, but some are now living right here in Phoenix.

How do you treat those Navajo people who live off the reservation? How does the Navajo Nation government treat them? It's going to have a bearing on what happens with the casino, the action of the tribal, state, and the federal government. They have to relive what Indian Health Service had to go through, and the BIA had to go through, when all of the Indian people started living off-reservation.

We also had a public hearing on the trust fund in 2003, and went to the local people—we went to the Five Agency Council. We went to off-reservation Navajo populations, such as Phoenix and Albuquerque. We had public hearings about the trust fund to educate the public about the Navajo Permanent Fund, and to get some suggestions as to its use. And the majority of those people, something like 82 percent of those people surveyed, and people who testified at those hearings said, "Leave it alone. Don't spend it."

Indian Casinos

Zah: There are Indian tribes that are very successful with their casinos. If you look at the leadership of those Indian tribes, the leadership may not quite agree with providing a per capita income for individual members of the tribe. However, they may be forced by the local people to divide tribal funds on a per person basis because they hear that some of the tribal members really want a portion of this money.

I guess you can look at this in two different ways. If you go along with per capita income, you then, in effect, give a message to the local people that you want to share this money with them each year. And that they really don't need to work for it or go to school and get their education. You don't really need to be motivated to do other things. It becomes a powerful message to members of the tribe that personal drive and incentives are diminished at the local level. The expectation to increase those benefits then become political, and that's how leaders are now elected.

Iverson: And the smaller the community, the more pressure there is likely to be for per capita payments. However, in a large tribe such as the Navajo, individual members would tend to receive a much smaller individual payment.

I took a group of students out to the Ak-Chin Indian Community yesterday. I've done that for a long time. Community members said they were so glad that they had decided not to take the per capita approach. This has given them more funding for housing for the elderly, and for fighting diabetes and taking on other issues.

Zah: Well, I think Ak-Chin is one of those small tribes that has resisted per capita income. They are a good model. As a group they decided to use their money on more housing, hospitals, health care, and children's education. I believe they are using their revenue in the most productive way for the people. And they do it with input from almost everybody on that small reservation.

People will get a larger amount of money if they are a member of a small tribe; it's an advantage. Now, up on the Navajo, we number about three hundred thousand. We will be approaching about half a million within the next twenty years. To have a per capita income,

even on a billion dollars, we're not going to get that much individu-
ally. And so I think it's in the best interests of the Navajo people that
these trust monies are kept intact and spent in the most expedient
way. And if there was a proposition for per capita income pending
before the Navajo Nation, I would be against it. I think we as Navajo
leaders need to guard against that. Because I'd like to see the Navajo
people continue to work hard for whatever little amount of money
that we get. As someone said, the Navajo people are hard-working
people, and we should remain that way.

Well, initially, way back in something like—in the mid-1980s,
when Indian people, tribal groups—tribes and groups elsewhere had
their casinos, Navajos kind of lagged behind, mainly because of two
or three issues. One of them was the stance between the states hav-
ing the authority to convene a compact and procedures between the
states and the Indian tribe. And the Navajo being the largest Indian
Nation in the United States, with a significant land base and numbers
of people living on-reservation, and then also many of them continu-
ing to be a traditional person, where some had limited education and
you just had to look at the composition of the Navajo.

The prevailing attitude was that we are not so sure if we want to
go into Indian gaming, because, number one, if we go to the state
of Arizona and ask them for a compact to do gaming on the Navajo,
then we are giving the state an inch, two inches to open the door, and
how do we know that they are not going to completely come in, open
that door fully so that they would begin having jurisdiction? So there
was that fear that once you submit yourself to agreeing with what
the state is doing for you—or maybe even with you—on the Navajo
reservation, among the Navajo people, then we are giving in to some
degree on our sovereignty. And so they looked at the issue that way.

The Navajo Nation is also blessed with natural resources. We
have the coal. We have the land base. We have all of these natural
resources on the Navajo Nation—the timber. And we have those,
and the Navajo people ought to develop that to gain more revenue
stream to the Navajo Nation government. In other words, those
natural resources are there to be developed, and if we get away from
that and then go into gaming, gaming is easy money. It's a no-
brainer. And all you had to do is you construct a building, and you
bring in your slot machine, put people to work, and it'll succeed.

It was that kind of economic development versus developing your own natural resources, where you had to use a lot of common sense, a lot of labor, a lot of people, skill in business management, and all of that in order for one to make money, that those were more challenging than just simply having gaming. So I have heard a lot of that kind of a discussion among the Navajo people. And I guess the third issue that to the Navajo people also was important, and which was the social effect that it'll have on the traditional Navajo life, and that we are going to have a lot of our people that may want to spend their spare time at the casino rather than, let's say, working their land, planting their corn, planting their food, tending business of their cattle, and all of their work that needs to be done. So they wanted a balance, and they thought that gaming might cause a lot of the social ills.

The Tribal Council passed a resolution back in the 1990s to have gaming. The council made it in such a way that they had already named communities, which community was going to get casinos: Chinle; Navajo, New Mexico; LeChee in Page, Arizona; Cameron, Arizona. In the legislation they approved, it already named all those sites. That really brought in a lot of fears, especially among the traditional people. They were saying that "hey, it's going to be in our community, and I don't know if I like that." And it was not set strategically like the way it's being planned right now.

So the biggest difference between that mid-1980 resolution to the resolution that was passed in 2009 or 2008 was that the building of the casinos is going to be strategically set along I-40, between Gallup, New Mexico, and Flagstaff. If you do those right, then you are—the people that would patronize the place would be tourists, people that drive on the I-40, and that they would be strategically set. I believe there is one or two being planned around Farmington, a highly populated area. They are doing a better job of strategically naming those places where it would make money, while before, the resolution that was passed in the mid-1990s was just saturating the place with casinos. I didn't think that it was going to work, and that it was going to be unworkable. Plus, to put up a casino costs a lot of money. Lots and lots of money. It's a very expensive proposition.

Iverson: With no guarantee of success?

Zah: At that time, we didn't have the money. So I vetoed the resolution because there wasn't enough thought, there wasn't enough

planning, there wasn't enough strategic planning and discussion among the Navajo people to do that. And I vetoed it, and I said, "We should put this before the public, and let the people decide what we should do, and that there should be more strategic planning involved in this whole thing." And so they, subsequent to that resolution that was passed in the mid-1990s, the Navajo people voted on it, and they rejected it. And so that was essentially what happened.

Iverson: Did they vote another time against it, too?

Zah: Well, I think they voted on it three times and then the last time, it passed. And it passed because they took care of some of those concerns that I had, which was better planning should be put in place, and probably they saw that we were beginning to have some extra revenues that were coming in. Now, the reason why I like what I see now is that in the year 2010, the Navajo Nation Gaming Enterprise, which is an enterprise of the Navajo government, went to the Investment Committee and the Budget and Finance Committee, and they have asked those two committees to approve a plan where they would use some of the monies that have been invested and have earned some significant amount of interest money.

What the gaming enterprise did is they asked the two committees, the budget and the investment committees, to borrow that to do their gaming. And they would pay back into the fund almost at the same rate as the going rate. I mean, the—what was considered adequate. I don't remember what those numbers were, but still, the Permanent Trust Fund would make money, because if you leave the Permanent Trust Fund sitting there in its present form at $1 billion, it earns a certain amount of interest, the money, additional money, that it generates each year. If you weigh that amount versus the money being used to build the casino, I think what they did is they went 1 or 2 percent above that, so that the Permanent Fund would still grow. It would bring in more money from gaming. And the beauty of all of that is they didn't have to go to the outside bank.

They didn't have to go to an outside bank and bring in, let's say, Wells Fargo, and Wells Fargo would end up making lots of money because they are financing the gaming development on the Navajo. So the gaming enterprise and the Navajo Nation were very smart in saving that money, putting money into a trust. And all of the revenues it generated, then they just simply borrowed money from

itself to do development. That's the beauty of it. And the guy who was the gaming director was quoted in the *Navajo Times* saying that he knew of no other tribe that was in a position to do that.

All of the other Indian gaming facilities were built using outside banks, and then the tribes indebted themselves to those banks, and some of them are being called because the casinos weren't doing very well. But they still had all this money indebted to the bank that they had to pay. With the Navajo Nation, they just borrowed from one pocket, and then maybe from several pockets to do what they wanted to do, with the idea that it was going to generate more revenues, and those monies would be put back and given back to the Navajo Nation. That's the beauty of it, and that's what you call "self-sufficiency." When we were putting the Permanent Trust Fund together way back twenty-seven years ago, that was the goal. That's why we did what we did: that we wanted to have Navajo Nation become, using that money, self-sufficient in the future.

Iverson: In its first year of operation, the Navajo Nation's Fire Rock Casino yielded significant profits. Although many casinos in the Southwest and elsewhere have struggled lately, Fire Rock has been a success from the start. Its performance has encouraged the Navajo Nation to approve five additional casinos in Northern Arizona and New Mexico.

Ninety percent of Fire Rock's revenue came from slot machines during its first year. If current trends continue, it is clear that the casinos will be a major source of revenue to the Navajo Nation, and their success will demonstrate the ability of the Navajos to operate this kind of enterprise.

The Navajos Are Lucky

Zah: The Navajo Nation has a new director of gaming, Bob Winter. He has a lot of experience in developing Indian gaming throughout the nation. And so I think those kinds of situations will be ironed out, probably, within the next couple of years.

And the Navajos are so lucky, because we live in three states. Whatever number of slot machines that might be brought into the Navajo, we're not going to get that from one particular state. For

example, in Arizona, the state allows Navajo to have something like 2,400 slot machines. And that's only on the Arizona side. I think on the New Mexico side, the Navajo can put any number as long as it's reasonable and is economically viable.

But that won't eat into the number of slot machines that they have coming from Arizona. We're lucky in the sense. We can have more machines than any of the other tribes, because our land extends into three states.

8

Tomorrows

"I Am Very Optimistic about the Navajo Future"

DURING THE YEARS OF PETERSON ZAH'S CHILDHOOD, most Navajo families led what observers called traditional lives. As described in Chapter 1, Peterson Zah learned from different members of his family, and he learned about responsibilities through caring for family livestock. Zah does not remember this time romantically. His family knew poverty and hunger, yet Zah clearly would not trade that experience for others that might be available today or tomorrow. Today, the average Navajo child grows up in town—either in communities situated on the reservation border or within the Navajo Nation itself. During many seasons of the year and many parts of the Navajo Nation, one can drive for hours and see very few sheep. That reality would have been almost unimaginable during his childhood, as is the reality of nearly two thousand American Indian students attending Arizona State University (ASU) today.

From 1995 to 2010, Peterson Zah served as a special advisor to the president of ASU in regard to American Indian concerns. Working with Lattie Coor and Michael Crow, Zah was ideally situated to help the university improve its record in terms of recruitment, retention, and graduation of Navajo and other Indian students.

Because he had attended ASU in the early 1960s, at a time when few Indians graduated from the university, Zah deeply cared about

these matters. But he wanted ASU to achieve a better record as well because Navajo success in college would have such a dramatic impact on the lives of individuals, the well-being of communities, and the future of the Navajo Nation.

Iverson: You've spoken about your childhood and growing up in a place like Low Mountain. I'm wondering if you could add something about living in a Navajo community today as compared to when you grew up.

Zah: Low Mountain, Pinon, and Black Mesa are the center of the Navajo Nation, because they are centrally located on the Navajo Nation, and not being so close to border towns surrounding the Navajo Nation. We probably represent the most traditional of all the Navajo groups. And certainly discussions about government, about education, about health, and all of those kinds of issues will take a different turn, and we'll discuss them in a different context than what other Navajo people may experience that are close to other rural and urban areas.

So I wouldn't say it was a difficult thing that we evolved through— let's say in the history of the development of communities like Pinon and Low Mountain and Black Mesa area. Everybody had a hard life. Maybe ours wasn't any harder than the other communities, but we managed. We managed to stick together; we managed to rally around issues to improve our living condition. And I could remember living in Low Mountain, and we practically had nothing. It was just hogan after hogan, people living there without any kind of infrastructure in that community. It wasn't until some of us that cared enough about communal life and what we wanted to have started working on building infrastructures so that a lot of developments would come to the community, such as highways, trading posts, schools, and health workers.

We were one of the very few chapters on the Navajo Nation that had a chapter house built towards the end. All of that happened because of the influx of educated youngsters. It's something that I take a lot of pride in. It was done by the people, and it was done at our own pace and in our own way. When you see something like that, you know that that is an expressed desire by the local people. When you see that happening, you know that the people had taken the time to go through the pains of suggesting those things.

They knew that they had to satisfy our own way of thinking. It had to satisfy our goals. And it certainly had to satisfy what we're trying to resolve here. They didn't always completely reject everything that other people had to offer to them. They took that under advisement. They looked at it, and they would critique it. And they hardly ever made any decision the same day that those suggestions were made to them. They took the time—they weighed all of the negatives and the positives to some of those suggestions. You had to hand it to a community that operates that way. Some people, non-Navajo people, may not like that. They may say it's too long, it's too cumbersome. But in the long run, it's a good thing that they did that. They always wind up doing the right thing if they take the time.

Violence among Navajos

Iverson: With urbanization, more Navajos live in urban environments where violent crime can occur. I remember that terrible incident down at the University of Arizona when a Navajo woman student killed another Navajo woman. That speaks, I think, to some of those issues about values and urbanization. There are so many more people now, not only who live off-reservation, but so many people within the reservation who live in town rather than out in the country. In the long term, it has to have some impact in terms of how things work and what language people speak, and other related issues.

Zah: Well, I never thought the day would come to the Navajo people when we would be doing such things to each other. It's here. It's among the Navajo people. I used to think that when I read the newspaper way back in the late 1940s, when I read about somebody murdering somebody in the city of Albuquerque or in Phoenix, and sitting back on the reservation I used to think that "well, all of those kinds of things happen in the city. And they're three or four hundred miles away." So you kind of ignore all of that and say, "It'll never happen—it'll never happen—never happen here on the Navajo, because there's a few of us and we don't think that way. We believe that every life is so important, so special, and so spiritual, that you don't do that to each other. And Navajos will never, ever do that."

But I was wrong. So were many other Navajo people. Those kinds of things are before us, right now.

Changing Lifestyles

To me, all that indicates is that the Navajo lifestyle is changing; Navajo culture is not static. It's changing—it's going to continue to change, because we may live way out there on the Navajo Nation where we don't have all of these modern conveniences, modern technology, and all of that. But sooner or later, all of what's around us is going to come in, because we continue to encourage the young people to go out and get an education. And if we don't have the educational facilities built for them on-reservation, they're going to have experience out here, for example, in Tempe and Phoenix and Albuquerque and other places—they're going to feel and taste the modern conveniences, the local stores, the banking and jobs and education, and all of those are readily made available to them. And they're going to get used to it.

So when they go back to the Navajo Nation, they're going to ask for some of those conveniences as well. And if the Navajo Nation government does not provide it, then those Navajo people are going to continue to stay out here, where they can get those things.

To me, that's what's happening right now. Because this surge of Navajo people living off-reservation just occurred within the last fifteen to twenty years. We're really feeling the influx of Navajo people and Navajo students coming off the reservation.

To some degree, you have to put that back on the shoulders of the Navajo leadership, because we continue to tell our students to get an education. Go out and get an education and be what you want to be. We're pushing them maybe a little bit too much in the direction of urging them to get a white man's education. Maybe what we, as the leaders of the Navajo Nation, should be saying is to get your local Navajo cultural education. All of the Navajo teachings, the Navajo values, the Navajo religion, Navajo lifestyle, and all of that make the Navajo people who they are. We should maybe be saying, "Learn that first and equip yourself with all of that learning while you are on the reservation at a young age. Then you go out—but only after

you have mastered what the Navajo people are all about. Then you can go out and learn about the white man's ways—but keep on remembering that you are not there to stay, that you are not there to fully embrace everything that they do. There are good sides and bad sides of both cultures, and your job is to select the things that are good for you, things that are good for the Navajo people."

We never really said that loudly. Yes, there have been suggestions, and there have been some people that were saying that. But we didn't really say that in unison as a concerted effort to tell our people that. So you have a situation now where many of these people come out here and they'll probably stay here.

Well, with the Navajo situation, it's an issue between the Office of the President and the council. And we have an eighty-eight-member council elected by the local people within those precincts throughout the Navajo nation. They have certain powers, responsibilities as council delegates, and they are fully exercising those powers that have been given to them by the Title 2 amendment. On the other hand, the Office of the President is questioning some of those powers, and perhaps even the exercise of those powers and the responsibilities.

Debate about the Council Size

That's the discussion between the two entities that led to this whole idea of trying to reduce the Navajo Nation Council from eighty-eight to twenty-four delegates. Back several years ago, the Navajo Nation had voted on tribal government reform to reduce the eighty-eight all the way down to twenty-four. In that voting, the Navajo people were given certain numbers. One was eighty-eight, and I think the other one was forty-eight or forty-four, or something like that, and then twenty-four. And the Navajo, through referendum vote, chose the twenty-four. But then the council came back, because they had the power to discuss those kinds of situations in their own council meeting. They came back, and they said that they had to have a supermajority, which meant that at each of the chapter houses, there has to be a majority that went for the twenty-four. They therefore discarded the simple majority, and although the twenty-four council delegates had won during that year, the Navajo Council still did not

accept that, and because their lawyer advised them that there had to be a supermajority. And so this time around, in the year 2010, the president essentially did the same thing, and it was a replay of what happened back then.

Iverson: This is President Joe Shirley?

Zah: Yes. And it was just a simple replay, but to have the rules also be decided first, and which was that there would be a simple majority that would have precedence over anything else. And so that's what happened, and as a result, a majority of the Navajo people voted for the twenty-four. And that raised a lot of questions. It was an eye-opener for political observers away from the Navajo and even on the Navajo Nation, and that the twenty-four council delegates, the suggestion of having twenty-four council delegates, won over the eighty-eight. The council fought very hard to maintain the eighty-eight, and—but the local people disagreed.

Now, subsequent to all of that, then came this whole idea about how do you then reapportion those twenty-four seats? That was left out in the open. Clearly, the council's responsibility was to overlook that, and then maybe come out with some kind of a reapportionment through the local election office, the election administration. But the president kind of beat them to the punch, because he was already working on some reapportionment plan—several reapportionment plans. And he took those reapportionment plans throughout the main chapters, agency governments, on the Navajo Nation, and had people look at it and discuss the reapportionment plan. And there was one or two, or even three that they liked from the local area. So what he did is that he just took those two or three that the people liked, and then came back together with his administration, and they presented one plan to the election office.

Then the election office agreed with the plan, and they approved the plan in terms of how the reapportionment throughout the Navajo Nation was to be drawn, those lines. So it was something that was very controversial. The president couldn't do that alone, and he had to go to court and challenge some of the position that was taken by the council. And then the council did the same thing. They didn't fully agree with what the president was doing. So the courts had to again bail out the Navajo government, as they did in 1989, when the chairman at that time was put on administrative leave.

In this situation, the year 2010, the same thing happened. The Navajo Nation Supreme Court came out and basically saved the Navajo government from complete chaos. When we were putting the Navajo Nation Supreme Court together way back in 1984 or beginning of 1983 and '84, we thought about that. We discussed all of those kinds of situations, and that we didn't want to see it again.

When you have people that are clubbing one another and they are hurting each other, you don't want to ever see and revisit those kinds of scenes. Because of that, it was important that we created a Navajo Nation Supreme Court where they would take on some of those issues. I was very proud the day that Navajo Nation Supreme Court made those rulings, because it set the record straight. The Navajo Nation Supreme Court looked at it in the legal way, in a very independent review, what was happening. We are now at a point where people are preparing, and in some cases, to run for those twenty-four seats that were announced.

That's where the Navajo Nation is right now. There will be a primary election, as I understand it, on August 24 this year, and then a general election will be on November 2. And then we will have a new twenty-four-member council, ready to be seated, and taking the oath of office at the inauguration in the middle of January 2011.

The Navajo people came together, putting pressure on the government. They were just tired of all of the publicity surrounding individual council delegates and how they were misleading the people, how they were really operating without any kind of strict accountability to the Navajo people. There was a lot of controversy over the manner in which they use Navajo people's money, in many cases to take care of their own personal things. They didn't like that. They got tired of all of that.

There is no magic thing to the number eighty-eight. And it was just through all these years, it got to that number, but there is nothing magic about that "eighty-eight." There is also nothing really magic about the twenty-four either.

Iverson: There has been some expression of concern on the part of some Navajo people who believe the reduction in members means that rural communities will be neglected. Other Navajos argue that the change will give greater voice to urban people and urban concerns in Shiprock and Chinle.

Zah: Well, I think in the reapportionment plan that I have seen thus far, they took an extra careful review of that issue. I think that's why they have—like before, when there were eighty-eight council members, areas like Shiprock, and Tuba City, and Fort Defiance would have anywhere from two, three, or even four council delegates from one community. And now, that didn't really work out to the advantage of the local community. In fact, many of them were just in each other's way. And they never were able to really get a lot done. So this time, when the council was reduced to twenty-four, those areas only got one, and so that they couldn't dominate the small, local chapters. They made it so that there was a balance between small chapters versus the big chapters. And that's some of the features of the new apportionment plan that Navajo will be using for voting in November 2010.

Iverson: One final question on this matter: do you think it will make any difference in regard to the number of women who are elected to the council? Will they be primarily hindered or helped by a different kind of number?

Zah: You know, I haven't really looked at that carefully—the number of women versus the men that are running for those twenty-four seats. But I think just by glancing over, the women will have their share. And I think in almost every precinct, you have a woman candidate, with the exception of maybe two, three, or four precincts. But you had some young ladies who aspired to become local leaders in November.

You never know. You never know what the overall development that's taking place will lead us to. It may be a situation years down the road where you're going to have more Navajo people living off the reservation and less back home. If that happens, we have all of those mineral resources. We have the coal, we have the natural gas, we have timbers, we have water—we have all of these things that we need that's on the reservation. And so Navajo have to be very careful that we don't leave all of those behind at home, and then come into Phoenix and then expect to live here all the rest of our lives.

We are approaching that day and age when we, as Navajo people, have to come together as a group, as an entity in trying to learn more about what we're doing, and what we're really doing to ourselves.

Iverson: Luci Tapahonso, in one of her poems, says, "We believe in old values and new ideas." But it's a tremendous challenge, isn't it? I mean, each generation faces its problems, but the whole impact of urbanization within the Navajo Nation is an area that is going to demand a lot more attention than it already has.

Zah: I guess Luci makes it sound very simple. And she's so right. We believe in old values and new ideas. Because if you look at the Navajo population, that's what it's all about. But I guess what I'm suggesting is that those old values—we as a Navajo Nation, in concert with one another as an entity, in a designed way, never really demonstrated that to the young people. Maybe we pushed them away from those old values and told them, "You should go out and get an education."

Transforming Education

It was hard to transform education from federal boarding schools away from the reservation back to the Navajo Nation on the Navajo reservation. I saw a gradual parental involvement that grew out of that federal policy of establishing schools on the Indian reservation. And it was a tough time period, where we saw, for example, for many years, the Navajo people were sending their children off-reservation. Many, many years, and I was a product of that. The parents never really had a role. They sent their kids away from the family environment nine months out of the year. The parents didn't have a say except for three months out of the year.

And then all of a sudden the federal government turned right around and said, "We're going to get ourselves out of educating the Indian students away from the reservation at boarding school. We're going to begin building schools back on your own territory, back on your own reservation. Now you have to learn how to participate in the running of schools and the teaching of your own children. And that's your responsibility." And the Navajo parents had a hard time dealing with that issue, because they really didn't know what the non-Indian people were saying to them, and why they were saying that.

There were some difficult times when the Navajo Nation began taking full control of its own educational institutions. People disagreed about the teaching of Navajo culture. In the past few years, I have visited various classes in various high schools including Greyhills Academy High School, Tuba City High School, Monument Valley High School in Kayenta, and Monument Valley High School in Utah, Shiprock High School, Window Rock High School, Ganado High School, Crownpoint High School, Tohatchi High School, Gallup High School, and Navajo Preparatory School in Farmington.

Clan Names

When you visit those high schools and talk to the students, when they introduce themselves, they don't introduce themselves only simply using their names. But the first thing they say is, "I am this clan. My father's clan is this, and my grandfather's clan and maternal grandma's clan is this." And that's the first thing they say—they say to me when they're in the process of introducing themselves. And then they say, "I want to go to your school at ASU and I want to know what kind of classes you offer, and what kind of scholarship and dormitory program do you have?" So that's the first thing that they tell you.

They're very proud of saying that. You could have never heard that thirty years ago. Navajo youngsters wouldn't tell you that—they wouldn't know. Because the whole educational institution and the system was trying to get them out of their Navajo-ness into modern white ways of life and education that they were imposing on the Indian students.

So by visiting these schools, that's what I hear. And the second thing they tell you about is cultural instructions and Navajo history. They may not know all the details, they may not know the dates, they may not know all the things that happened specifically to the Navajo people, but they know there is a Navajo history.

Now, the Navajo Nation is making great progress. If we keep that up for the next ten, twenty, thirty years, we're going to really have a nation unto itself. A nation that is self-determined really understands where it has been, and a nation that understands where it wants to go. I think that the Navajos have a future.

We hear a lot about drug involvement; yes, we hear a lot about alcohol and the meth that has gone onto the Navajo Nation among the youth. You know, those are man-made things. Those are problems—they're also challenges. And I think on the meth controversy among the Navajo, the Navajo people really rose up in arms, the last two or three years, and they're really fighting it very effectively. So it's going to take those kinds of community involvement to get these kinds of terrible things that are happening to the Navajo people and local schools and local community—it's up to them to get rid of that. No one's going to get rid of them for them. And so they're basically involved in effectively dealing with that.

Community Cohesiveness

So there's a lot of community cohesiveness, based on what is happening at the local school. Many, many of the community activities really revolve in many cases around the school, and what the school is able to achieve. And I'll give you one or two good examples. In the 1970s and 1980s, when the Navajo people in Tuba City began taking full control of their local schools at Tuba City High, they went all the way in supporting their local sports program. I remember going to high school basketball games and football games, and I remember going to cross-country and track meets. Those kids were so proud of themselves.

The Tuba City High School women's basketball team took the state championship maybe four or five times during that twenty-year or fifteen-year period. They often played that state tournament here, at the America West Arena, where the Phoenix Suns professional basketball team plays. Navajo people would come in large numbers—fans, families, relatives—and they would fill that place up with Navajo supporters. And it was very hard for the people here in Phoenix to understand that—to understand why the Navajo people would drive three hundred miles to come to support their high school basketball team.

There's a big community pride with a tremendous amount of support for the local school in those communities. They love their grandchildren. They'll go any distance—how far they drove didn't

matter. How much it cost to get there didn't matter. The fact was that they wanted to support their school and they wanted to support their children. And so that's what happens—that's what happens when you educate and motivate the parents enough, so that they go all the way to support the activities of their local sports program.

Now, let's transfer that over to the city of Phoenix. I live in a school district here in Phoenix, and it's a big 5A school. They don't get that number at their basketball games, even at the state meet tournament. They don't get that number. And, you know, there are probably one thousand or two thousand at the most that I have seen by non-Indian teams. But with Navajo, it's not unusual to see fourteen thousand or fifteen thousand people at these games. I think people should just learn from that—that when you get the Indian people involved in supporting some worthwhile things like basketball games and supporting their children, they go out 100 percent and support that.

And I'm only using Tuba City as an example. Well, that happened with Window Rock High School, that happened with Monument Valley High School, and this year with Ganado—the girls' basketball team went all the way and took the state championship. It's something that the Navajo people are very proud of.

If you look at New Mexico, look what Shiprock High School did back in the '70s, you know, when they had that tremendous basketball team, and the whole community of Shiprock going over to the Pit in Albuquerque, where the University of New Mexico Lobos basketball team plays. During the state tournament, that place is just full to capacity with Navajo supporters. And it was something to see.

Commitment to Achievement

Zah: And for me, as an educator and as an observer, what the Navajo people are really sold on is this self-determination. I'm using only sports programs as an example. I'm following one of the things that's happening in the last two years. For example, last night I was reading about the spelling bee that just took place at the national level here about a week, two weeks ago. And there were some Navajo kids that went all the way—that went all the way to Washington, D.C.

They participated. Sure, they lost out and they got eliminated in the second round or so, you know, but the thing about it is that we're up there. We're up there. We're on the verge of having one of our Navajo youngsters become a national champion in the spelling bee program and contest.

So it's the Navajo people, and the Navajo children are the future of the Navajo Nation. And they're doing all of these things because the Navajo parents are giving them that desire and support that they really need to do something very well in the community. The Navajo kids are very proud of doing all of those things. Look at what happened in the community of Pinon, where you have a young Navajo eighth grader, Garrett Yazzie, and what he was able to invent to help out his mother to reduce her electricity bill by inventing a water heater, and a gadget that he used to heat his home—his trailer. Then ABC television came out in May and built him this nice beautiful home for him and his mother. That's going to get a lot of national attention, and people are going to view that in terms of what this young Navajo boy was able to invent, just simply because he was really dedicated to his mother and dedicated to looking at the overall problem the Navajo Nation faces.

What Garrett Yazzie has done is not going to stop there. Because the home that they built for him is an all-green home. That home is recycling its own water—self-contained. It's recycling its own water, and the water that they recycle is used to irrigate the little grass and other flowers that the family is growing outside of their home. And then they have solar—a solar panel that generates electricity. They have a wind panel that also generates electricity. And as I understand it from the engineers that helped design that facility here at ASU, the solar panel plus the wind-generated power, that will produce enough to take care of their home throughout the year.

There's going to be excess power that NTUA is going to buy from him—the Navajo Tribal Utility Authority, the organization that provides electrical services to homes on the Navajo Nation. And Garrett Yazzie, this eighth-grade kid and now a ninth-grade high school student, made a commitment by saying that "I would like to have all of my excess electricity to go to my neighbors—my uncle and my aunts and my grandma and my grandpa." And so even at that young age, he has such a responsibility towards his own relatives and

his own community. Whatever he invented, he was passing it around to get the results of what he was able to come up with.

When I see something like that happen, that's the future of the Navajo Nation. We don't have any indication right now—for all we know the Navajo Nation may start demanding that their homes be built with solar systems, with wind-powered, electric-producing machinery to heat their homes. We may not necessarily need all that much energy that gets produced by using the coal.

So the invention and the creation of what Garrett Yazzie did, to me is also unlimited. We haven't really seen the full recognition and the full potential of what this kid has, in terms of what he has in mind and in terms of helping the Navajo people and the way that we live. And so that only indicates to me that the Navajo people really have what it takes to survive—what it takes to do good and do well in taking care of the other members of their family.

I just wanted to add these pieces of information that I observed on the Navajo, and it really goes along the lines of self-determination. To have a nation that we can be proud of, we need more activities that are fully supported by the Navajo parents and Navajo students.

I wanted to add a little more to our discussion about self-determination. I used the example of basketball success at Tuba City and other schools around the Navajo, and then I also used the success of the spelling bee contestant from Chinle Public School—a person that went all the way to the national contest in Washington, D.C. And I want to add the third one, which is that we are now beginning to see more and more Navajo students come into colleges and university. I'll use what has happened here at ASU just as an example—a shining example of what could be. And that is in contrast to the numbers when I enrolled here at ASU, we had something like 672 Native American students. The president of Arizona State University, Lattie Coor, was telling me that we were stuck at that number—we could never go higher than that. We did everything we can under the sun to try to recruit more people, but we're just failing, or doing something wrong. And we can't seem to add any more to it. He just gave me the instruction that "let that be your concern. I can't tell you how you should resolve it, but let that be your concern—worry about it, and see how we can improve."

Recruitment and Retention

Well, I got involved in recruitment. And using a completely differ-ent model, different tactics, different ways of recruiting. Going to these high schools on the Navajo Nation, getting on the radio, and saying things publicly in the newspaper, then actually going into the classroom to talk to the students. Those made a big difference. Then on occasion I would get on the radio to talk to the Navajo parents about how important education is.

As a result of all of that, after something like ten years later, we now have approximately 1,500 Native American students that attend ASU. That's almost tripling the numbers in the 1995–96 year. And I believe that we're not going to stop there. We're going to keep on going—we're going to keep on recruiting more Native American students. My personal goal is to get to 2,000. Once we get to 2,000, that's still not going to be enough. So someone has to continue doing what we started here.

I see a lot of young Navajo people who are going to school—the recent graduates of ASU that are kind of following suit, that I'm working with. They are fully committed to this. And those young people, they make me happy, because I know at some point I'm going to start thinking about retirement. And it's good to look back and see that these young people are really, really serious about the continuation of getting more Native American students, more Navajo students to come into these colleges and universities.

And my prejudice is not only for ASU—I always told people that any university, whether it's Northern Arizona University, University of Arizona, Brigham Young University, University of Oklahoma, the University of Southern California, or any other community college, college, or university. It doesn't matter, as long as they get the expe-rience. And that's what we're looking for. So that was something that is also in line with the self-determination movement exhibited by the Indian students, and more particularly the Navajo students.

The second point I wanted to make is this: when I came on cam-pus, the retention rate of Native American students was so low. I remember the president telling me that "for every one hundred stu-dents we get one year, the following year, we lose one-half. We only have 50 percent—about 50 percent retention rate." He was saying

Peterson Zah meets with students.

that on a bad year, we lose 60 percent of the students that we gained the year prior. So that's a big concern.

We have begun a Native American achievement program. We started working with students in a different way, providing a different attitude. We are doing a lot with our faculty, with our staff so that they understand the American Indian students here. That added tremendously to the retention rate of the American Indian students. Then with the Native American Achievement Program, we got more mentors. American Indian graduate students are helping the undergraduates. Those activities are necessary to have your program succeed.

We got the retention rate all the way up to 78 percent, from 50 percent. That's a huge increase. Unfortunately, that 78 goes up and down. Some years we may have 70 percent, some years we may go back down to 68 percent, but then some years it goes back up to 77, and so on. We're trying to evaluate the program, and what we do from year to year.

We also asked for all those Navajo students who made 3.00 or above during that year. After we put the Native American Achievement Program into practice that year, we gained a clear picture of the Navajo students who were doing very well. And somewhere around 2003, we asked for the same number from the department

that deals with those issues here on campus. They gave us an increase of American Indian students who are making 3.00 and above. That number that they gave us was 144. That's a tremendous increase.

When I look at these three points, working here at ASU, the future just looks bright. If we can do that for the next ten years, the real progress is going to start happening on the American Indian reservations here throughout the Southwest. This whole thing is about self-determination, about having your local schools back in your home community, on your reservation, and having the Indian people come back into those classrooms as teachers, as model teachers, as mentors and role models. Those seem to be working very, very well. So I see those bright eyes every time I go into a classroom, and I always think to myself, my God, these are the students that are so smart, that are going to go back to the Navajo Nation. And they're going to be more fully equipped than I ever was. And when I went back to the Navajo Nation, I wasn't fully prepared. I was not ready. I didn't have the ammunition that they now have. And so these kids that are going back onto the reservation, or even that are going to be here in the city, they're fully equipped. They're going to have a wonderful life. And as a grandfather, that really encourages me and is an inspiration. It provides energy that I look towards from day to day.

We are one of the very few American Indian tribes where we live, truthfully live, our culture from day to day. And we certainly use at a high rate our language and communication not only among the local people but in other institutions like colleges and universities.

Revitalization

I think the language is being revitalized. The students now know the names of their clans. Now, for me that does something. There's a tremendous pride in that individual. Number two, there's a great desire to relearn the Navajo language if they were ever in the process of beginning to lose it. This creates a lot of cohesiveness among the Navajo people. And this is their language, this is their culture, this is their lifestyle.

We are trying to recruit more students to come to ASU. And our college kids have encouraged the high school students to learn their

language and culture. They also realize the importance of taking care of the elderly and the young. If it is anything that we agree on it is the importance of the language. There is tremendous pride in our ability to increase the reservation land base. This is something that really keeps us together.

Women in Politics

Only recently have Navajo women become more involved in Navajo politics. Yes, there were some good, able, capable Navajo women that ran for the council in the last several elections and several have been elected to represent their community, but they really did not have any major impact on the political system on the reservation.

But Lynda Lovejoy was one of those individuals who took a look at what was happening, and then decided to run. Despite all of the pessimism that passed her way—that was thrown her way—she stuck with her objectives. She was vigilant. She wanted to prove people wrong. And Linda is a fine individual. She's a good thinker. But she lacked experience.

I only wish that she would have taken some more time to analyze the situation that she was getting into, and maybe have the benefit of—I wouldn't say a better or anything like that, but wise advice from Navajo politicians that really know the business and that she would have been better prepared on the major issues. You can know the issues, but you have to know how to say them.

We're going to have more women probably running for the top office on Navajo Nation. Maybe more of them will make a concentrated effort to be elected to the council. A lot of able, capable young ladies are commanding those leadership posts out in the community.

Community and Individual Empowerment

Iverson: I've often thought about your particular upbringing in that stretch of territory between Keams Canyon and Low Mountain and your sense about the chapter house, and the fact that you didn't want

Window Rock to be the only place where they were making decisions. It seems to me that you have been dedicated to empowering the local chapters. When you became the chairman, you didn't want to be the imperial president. You wanted to make sure the local people had a say in what was going on. Is that a correct assumption on my part?

Zah: Yes. I would say that is probably a correct assumption, because it is something that I was involved in right from the beginning. I mean, I cared about people—I was very well-versed in the hardship that most people went through. I also knew about the needs and the desires of individuals that live out in the community of Low Mountain. And I knew that, if given the opportunity, many of the people that I grew up with would take advantage of those opportunities. Sometimes you have to be mindful of the fact that when you present those opportunities to individuals, that many will take advantage of those opportunities. Those individuals are able to function very well in their community, or even on or off the reservation because they saw how important those opportunities were. And one of those opportunities was going out of your community to receive your education, and then using that education to better not only your own family, but the community. The Navajo Nation, for example, can benefit from that.

I spent a lot of my lifetime defending the rights of the individual, because I knew that if given some opportunities, these individuals would surface somewhere to become leaders of the Navajo Nation. I guess that's the reason I'm here at Arizona State University— because I see a lot of good qualities in young people, Navajo people that come through colleges and universities here in the Valley. When I see one of those students, I always work with them in such a way that they understand that they have a duty to go back to their home communities, wherever they came from, to serve the people.

Iverson: If you think about the people from the Navajo Nation who come here to school, the numbers are really remarkable. When you were finishing up at ASU, I bet if somebody said to you, "Forty-six years from now there will be more than eight hundred Navajo students at ASU rather than eight," you would probably have been pretty skeptical that that day would ever come. And yet here we are. You've had a major role in bringing that about, in terms of working with the admissions staff and financial aid and things like that. This is a

big university, and it's a lot to take on in terms of seeing the concrete, positive results. Not everybody is a success story. But what I find myself saying to Navajo students—the key message is one of empowerment. Saying, "You can do it." You have to believe in yourself, but this is an opportunity. I've seen person after person accept that challenge, and at the end of the year in Neeb Hall or wherever we are, when you're speaking about the people who are graduating or going on, that has to be an evening of particular pride and emotion for you.

Zah: Well, that all came about because I had a vision. I had a dream of my own, that if we educate more youngsters on the Navajo reservation they would rise to the occasion, become self-sufficient, and solve their own problems. And the way to get to that stage is to recruit those students who are able, capable, and with good character, good academic record, that see all of this as an opportunity—if you can get those individuals to a university and then begin working with them, that is something that I wanted to do and wanted to promote and implement here at ASU.

In other words, when I came here to ASU in 1995, one of the things that I was told was that the university was really interested in getting more Indian students. Well, I had to figure out, how do you get more students? And then I started going out into the communities, seeing and talking to different tribal government leaders within the state here, as well as in the Southwest, and started recruiting students. And when you start dealing with those numbers, you have to set a goal for yourself. That's when we sat down and said, "By the year 2015, we've got to have two thousand American Indian students here on campus." And it's a goal that we set for ourselves. That's something to work for every day. You have to say, "Today, I've got to recruit so many more students to come to ASU."

If we can have Indian youngsters come to ASU, and then put them back on the reservation upon graduation, many of those problems will come to its own resolution by its own people. We can't always expect somebody to come in from somewhere and start working on those problems for us. It has to be done from within. And those are American Indian students that have an opportunity to blossom into powerful leaders. That's the only way that we can effectively resolve those issues.

Iverson: In American society, many people remain uncertain about education, and what it will bring, and whether it will take

people away from you. I think you and others deserve a lot of credit for your determination to set a course that would be productive. I can't walk across the ASU campus at any time of the day without seeing Navajo people. I believe your work here has made a difference.

Zah: Well, that's a wonderful thing to see. I do the same thing. I went to school here at Arizona State University in the early 1960s. And when you walked across campus, you didn't see anybody that was Native.

And nowadays, I walk across the campus, and it's not unusual, for example, to go from my office over to the law school and along the way have three individuals that stop you, and they want to shake hands and they want to introduce themselves and talk. And those are our own people. Those are our own American Indian students. And the same thing happens when I go from my office over to the president's office or over to the football stadium. It's not unusual to see three to five people that stop you and introduce themselves as individuals who come from your tribe. And it gives me a great feeling, a lot of satisfaction.

Accomplishments

Iverson: I saw a publication about ASU and looking towards the future. And you're rather prominently featured in this overview. Moreover, you have been honored by Arizona State University through an honorary degree presented to you at the spring commencement in 2005. How do you feel about that kind of recognition?

Zah: Well, those are things that you don't actually seek out, to be in that position, or to be mentioned in those kinds of either newspapers or booklets or magazines. But when you work long and hard and long enough, you know, people recognize what's happening. And I think the discussion that we're having today is one of those where people are beginning to realize the significance of American Indian students' presence here at Arizona State University. And the magazine that you're referring to is just recognizing the fact that a lot of the work that was done was done by me and others. And I cannot really take all of the credit for it by myself. There were so many people that had a role in bringing many of these students to the campus here.

Peterson Zah is awarded an honorary degree by his alma mater, Arizona State University, in 2005. Peterson Zah's mother Mae Zah is at his right.

The Navajo culture, as we all know, is not static. It doesn't remain unchanged for years and years. It has already gone through a lot of transformation. Our belief systems have changed; the way we speak and the way we do business have changed. Our lifestyle has changed. Everything that Navajo people do from day to day has changed. And you can point at things like transportation—we're no longer using horses to get to places.

We're no longer using wagons to get where we want to go. We're using pickup trucks and we're using cars, and some of the tribal officials are using airplanes. So our mode of travel has changed. And you can't really knock old ideas, such as the concept of walking to where you want to go. Since we walked because we didn't have the transportation, it really kept us healthy. We didn't have to put up with diabetes. The old ways were good to the Navajo people. Traditional language and lifestyle and history, those were all good to the Navajo people. I don't think that we should completely abandon those ideas, because we made them part of our culture. I think that Navajo people need to look at themselves individually and analyze what they're going through, and try to retain some old values.

Iverson: Are you optimistic about the Navajo future?

Zah: I'm very optimistic. I'm very optimistic, perhaps because I work with the young people. They are talking about new ideas and new ways of doing things. So when I experience that, I am highly optimistic about our future.

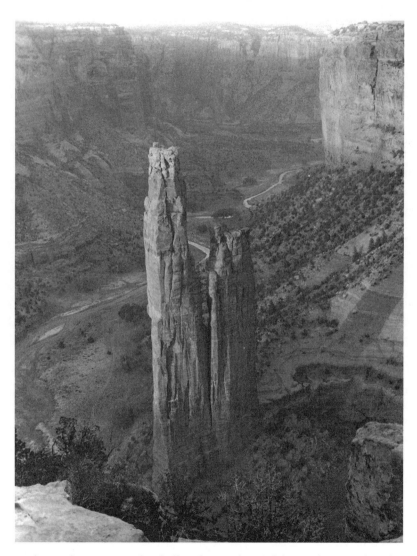

Spider Rock in Canyon de Chelly. This is a beautiful site of great cultural significance, where Spider Woman taught Changing Woman how to weave.

Epilogue

Restoring Harmony

Iverson: On November 9, 2010, Peterson Zah wrote to Arizona State University president Michael Crow officially informing him of his intention to resign his position, effective November 30. Zah had served as a special advisor to the ASU president for the previous fifteen years. As this chapter emphasizes, he had been pleased to have the opportunity to work with students, staff, and faculty to build programs to empower American Indian individuals and communities.

At the same time, Zah had missed Diné Bikéyah (Navajo country), and he missed particular people from his hometown area of Window Rock. Moreover, given his years with the DNA People's Legal Services program and as chairman and president of the Navajo Nation, part of him missed the different cadence of daily demands.

Several years ago at the conclusion of one of our discussions, I had asked him whether he had missed any of the Window Rock scene. "It's not that you've totally left it," I ventured, "but you're not on the council floor every day. Do you miss that kind of engagement? Do you miss that kind of fighting?" Zah replied, "I don't miss all of that, but I miss the Navajo people. . . . There's a difference between the two," he added. "It's just one of those things when you get into something, you know that's what you want to do."

I thought about this exchange when I learned about Zah's resignation and his decision to join with others to establish Restore Harmony. On its website in November 2010, Restore Harmony introduced itself as "a large group of friends and family members of Peterson and Rosalind Zah." It then declared: "In light of the current situation causing turmoil and frustration within the Navajo Nation government, economy, education systems, and the health of our communities, we have formed a group that aims to inspire a

positive change within these realms." Restore Harmony pledged to "focus our efforts toward the future and visualize a positive change on the Navajo Nation." "If we don't act now," it concluded, "the future generations of our people will be depleted in culture, language, traditions, community, faith, and all that enables us to live in harmony and balance. That is what motivates us to make a positive change within the Navajo Nation for our people today and for the generations and generations yet to come."[1]

In his letter to Crow, Zah reiterated that during his years at the university he had "conveyed the message to many students to return to their tribal communities after graduation to help their people. After careful consideration," he added, "I am now challenged by my own statements and beliefs to return . . . to help restore peace, harmony, respect, and dignity amongst the Diné Nation." Next month he would celebrate his 73rd birthday. Members of his generation usually had been part of the kind of extended family in which Zah had been raised. But the members of the Navajo Nation Council as well as the president and vice president of the Navajo Nation in the more recent past had come from backgrounds that not only varied from his experience but also from each other.

The 2010 election for president and vice president of the Navajo Nation did not turn out as many observers had anticipated. Lynda Lovejoy ran again for president, and this time she did not face an incumbent as she had in 2006. Rex Lee Jim, a Princeton-educated poet from Rock Point, sought to become vice president if Ben Shelly became president. Lovejoy and Shelly both hailed from New Mexico, and so it appeared certain that someone from the Land of Enchantment would gain the top position in Navajo government for the first time in seventy years.

In the presidential primary election in August, Lovejoy came in first, and the way seemed to be clear to triumph in November. However, the so-called Lovejoy landslide failed to materialize, and Vice President Ben Shelly won by over three thousand votes. Several factors contributed to Shelly's victory. Serving as vice president provided him with valuable experience and name recognition. Choosing Rex Lee Jim to be his vice presidential running mate broadened his overall base. And, finally, some Navajos opposed any woman becoming president because they believed that women's participation in

politics would lead inevitably to internal division and difficulty. This conclusion was based on an interpretation of Navajo creation stories. Although most Navajos did not share this interpretation, those who did obviously could not support Lovejoy.

However, a more sizable bloc of voters expressed their unhappiness about politicians not paying sufficient attention to traditional Navajo values. Peterson Zah was, in fact, not alone in reemphasizing the importance of gaining a good education, speaking the Navajo language, honoring the concepts of *k'é* and *hozho*, and recognizing the significance of the clan system.

Rex Lee Jim and Herb Yazzie numbered among those who stressed the significance of these elements. A two-term council member from Rock Point, Jim also had sought the presidency of the Navajo Nation in 2010. He finished fourth in the primary election, but then was selected as Shelly's running mate and thus became vice president following the November election. Jim had grown up in the Rock Point community and had graduated from Princeton University in 1986. He then returned home to take on a variety of assignments for Rock Point and Diné College. Jim's command of written as well as spoken Navajo, his incisive analysis of key issues confronting the people, and his keen sense of humor all proved to be political attributes. "The Navajo Nation needs to proclaim itself to be a sovereign nation, and we need to act like a sovereign nation," Jim declared.[2]

In "What Is a Nation?" a presentation given in January 2011 at Arizona State University's Sandra Day O'Connor College of Law, Navajo Nation Supreme Court Chief Justice Herb Yazzie articulated the importance of place. He, too, had completed a long journey, having earned his law degree from the Arizona State University law school. While recent months had revealed the challenges many Navajos faced in regard to their identities, Yazzie observed, those members of the Navajo Nation who had grown up working on the land, speaking the language, and learning from different generations usually did not worry about who they were.

However, Yazzie added, that anxiety was more likely to face those who had grown up apart from the land, who did not speak Navajo, and who had not learned from the elders. This sizable group included not only people who had grown up in distant cities or in reservation border towns like Gallup and Flagstaff but also a growing number

of people who resided in town within the Navajo Nation and who were less likely to have learned the Navajo language and frequently had been separated from the workings of Navajo culture.[3]

Securing the Future

As these pages have summarized, this situation eventually prompted Peterson Zah to resign his position at Arizona State University. Zah felt compelled to address this escalating turmoil and believed to do so more effectively he needed to return to a primary residence within the Navajo Nation.

This book went to press in early 2011, and this schedule obviously limited the degree to which we could address ongoing developments. We also realized the need for historical context. Throughout their history, the Navajos had demonstrated time and again their ability to adapt, to adjust, to change, to incorporate, and to continue. In the late nineteenth and early twentieth centuries, they had been seen as temporary occupants of the Southwestern stage. In the words of photographer Edward Curtis, the Navajos were assumed to be a "vanishing race," "passing into the darkness of an unknown future."[4]

However, the Navajos saw history not as something that happened to them but as something they made. The Navajo Treaty of 1868 returned only a fraction of their land base, but it did at least allow the people to go home. Thus, the treaty encompassed triumph as well as tragedy. Navajo leaders worked diligently through the years to add millions of acres to that initial land base. The Navajo population has also expanded dramatically, to a point that we can say with some confidence there are more Navajos today than there were Indians a century ago. Of course demographic growth and the expansion of a land base do not guarantee peace or prosperity; indeed, the considerable contingent entering the labor market each year poses perennial problems for the Navajo economy. Nevertheless, even given the dilemmas of the present, we can appreciate why Peterson Zah is ultimately optimistic about his people's future.

His response to the current challenges facing the Navajo Nation again encouraged Navajo empowerment. In turn, he drew strength from his family and his friends. He obtained inspiration from

traditional teachings. And he maintained his sense of obligation to the land itself.

At a presentation at the Heard Museum in the spring of 2010, Peterson Zah noted the investment the Navajo Nation had made in its young people. "We will need these young people," he continued, "to help build educational institutions and economic institutions, to run our governments, to teach our children's children. We have taken back the responsibility for setting the course for our children's education. We do this in anticipation of the day when they return to us and take upon themselves this same responsibility for their own children. That is how we will secure our future."[5]

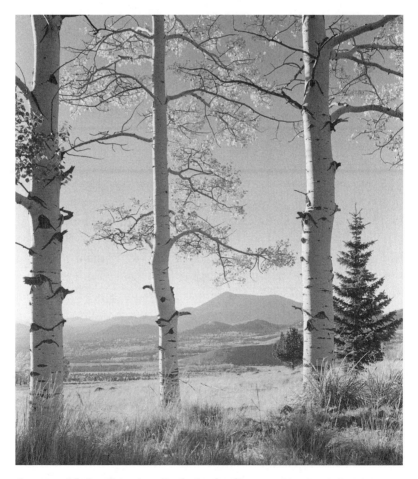

Aspens with San Francisco Peaks in the distance.

Appendix

Chairmen of the Navajo Tribal Council and Presidents of the Navajo Nation

Chairmen	Terms
Henry Chee Dodge	1923–1928
Deshna Clah Chischillige	1928–1932
Thomas Dodge	1932–1936
Marcus Kanuho (interim)	1936–1936
Henry Taliman	1937–1938
Jacob C. Morgan	1938–1942
Henry Chee Dodge	1942–1946
Sam Ahkeah	1946–1954
Paul Jones	1955–1963
Raymond Nakai	1963–1970
Peter MacDonald	1970–1983
Peterson Zah	1983–1987
Peter MacDonald	1987–1989
Leonard Haskie (interim)	1989–1991

Presidents	Terms
Peterson Zah	1991–1994
Albert Hale	1995–1998
Thomas Atcitty	1998
Milton Bluehouse (interim)	1999
Kelsey Begaye	1999–2003
Joe Shirley Jr.	2003–2011
Ben Shelly	2011–

Notes

Introduction

1. For an overview of the first era, see Peter Iverson, *Diné: A History of the Navajos* (Albuquerque: University of New Mexico Press, 2002), 1–33.

2. Stefani Salkeld, *Southwest Weaving: A Continuum* (San Diego, CA: San Diego Museum of Man, 1996), 11; Joe Ben Wheat, "Rio Grande, Pueblo, and Navajo: Cross-Cultural Influences," in Nora Fisher, ed., *Rio Grande Textiles* (Santa Fe: Museum of New Mexico Press, 1994), 22. See also Arthur Woodward, "Romance of Navajo Silver," *Arizona Highways* (1944), 32–37.

3. See Thomas D. Hall, *Social Change in the Southwest, 1350–1815* (Lawrence: University Press of Kansas, 1989), 134–164.

4. AnCita Benally, "Hané'Béé'ééhaniíh: With Stories It Is Remembered" (master's thesis, Arizona State University, 1993).

5. Gerald Thompson, *The Army and the Navajo: The Bosque Redondo Reservation Experiment, 1863–1868* (Tucson: University of Arizona Press, 1976).

6. Luci Tapahonso, "In 1864," in Luci Tapahonso, *Sáanii Dahataał: The Women Are Singing* (Tucson: University of Arizona Press, 1993), 10.

7. For Navajo accounts of the Long Walk era, see Ruth Roessel, ed., *Navajo Stories of the Long Walk Period* (Tsaile, AZ: Navajo Community College Press, 1973).

8. For an overview of this second era, see Iverson, *Diné*, 33–65.

9. Evangeline Parsons Yazzie and Edward T. Begay presentations at the Navajo Treaty Day Commemoration Program, June 1, 1999, Northern Arizona University, Flagstaff, Arizona. Notes by Iverson on presentations.

10. For an overview of the third era, see Iverson, *Diné*, 66–136.

11. "Chee Dodge Addresses the Problems That Would Occur with the End of Trust Status and the Division of Tribal Land," February 2, 1914, in Peter Iverson, ed., *"For Our Navajo People": Diné Letters, Speeches & Petitions, 1900–1960* (Albuquerque: University of New Mexico Press, 2002), 4–5.

12. Iverson, *Diné*, 110–112.

13. Ibid., 117–125.

Chapter 1. Generations

1. Luci Tapahonso, "This Is How They Were Placed for Us," in Luci Tapahonso, *Blue Horses Rush In: Poems and Stories* (Tucson: University of Arizona Press, 1997), 39–42.

2. Tapahonso, "A Birthday Poem," in Tapahonso, *Blue Horses Rush In*, 79–80.

3. "Ned Hatathli Notes the Altered Place of Livestock in the Navajo Economy," September 19, 1957, in Peter Iverson, ed., *"For Our Navajo People": Diné Letters, Speeches & Petitions, 1900–1960* (Albuquerque: University of New Mexico Press, 2002), 250–252.

4. "David Clah Categorizes Sheep as a Thing of the Past," February 19, 1947, in Iverson, *"For Our Navajo People,"* 237–238.

5. "Tom Dodge Says the Tribal Council Must Deal with Traders, Soil Erosion, and Missionaries," October 30, 1933, in Iverson, *"For Our Navajo People,"* 166–169.

6. "Roger Davis Calls for the Navajos to Receive the Same Kind of Benefits as Non-Indian Farmers and Ranchers," June 6, 1940, in Iverson, *"For Our Navajo People,"* 135–137.

Chapter 2. Schools

1. "Sam Gorman Speaks about the Value of a Good Education," February 2, 1941, and November 4, 1953, in Peter Iverson, ed., *"For Our Navajo People": Diné Letters, Speeches & Petitions, 1900–1960* (Albuquerque: University of New Mexico Press, 2002), 94–99.

2. Peter Iverson, *Diné: A History of the Navajos* (Albuquerque: University of New Mexico Press, 2002), 159.

3. See, for example, Ann Nolan Clark, *Little Herder in Autumn* (Phoenix, AZ: Bureau of Indian Affairs, 1940).

Chapter 3. Leaders

1. Jennifer Nez Denetdale, *Reclaiming Diné History: The Legacies of Navajo Chief Manuelito and Juanita* (Tucson: University of Arizona Press, 2007), 84.

2. "Ned Hatathli Urges the Tribal Council to Plan for the Future," October 14, 1955, in Peter Iverson, ed., *"For Our Navajo People": Diné Letters, Speeches & Petitions, 1900–1960* (Albuquerque: University of New Mexico Press, 2002), 198–199.

Chapter 4. Lawyers

1. Peter Iverson, *Diné: A History of the Navajos* (Albuquerque: University of New Mexico Press, 2002), 207–209.

2. Peter Iverson, *The Navajo Nation* (Albuquerque: University of New Mexico Press, 1983), 33–34.

3. "Annie Wauneka Analyzes the Job Being Done by the General Counsel," January 23, 1956, in Peter Iverson, ed., *"For Our Navajo People"*: *Diné Letters, Speeches & Petitions, 1900–1960* (Albuquerque: University of New Mexico Press, 2002), 200–202.

Chapter 5. Traders

1. Adams, William Y. *Shonto: A Study of the Role of the Trader in a Modern Navajo Community.* Smithsonian Institution, Bureau of American Ethnology, Bulletin 188 (Washington, D.C.: Government Printing Office, 1963).

2. Peter Iverson, *Diné: A History of the Navajos* (Albuquerque: University of New Mexico Press, 2002), 217.

3. Peter Iverson, "Building toward Self Determination: Plains and Southwestern Indians in the 1940s and 1950s," *Western Historical Quarterly* (April 1985), 172–173.

Chapter 7. Resources

1. LeNora Begay Trahant, *The Success of the Navajo Arts and Crafts Enterprise: A Retail Success Story* (New York: Walker & Company, 1996), 13–22.

2. Mireya Navarro, "Navajos Hope to Shift from Coal to Wind and Sun," *New York Times*, October 25, 2010.

Epilogue

1. Restore Harmony website, http://www.restoreharmony.net. The board of directors for Restore Harmony as of October 5, 2011, included Dr. Manley Begay Jr., Kimberly Kanuho, Helen Store, Henry Barber, Flora Nez, and Peterson Zah.

2. Rex Lee Jim's life and career are considered in Mark E. Bernstein, "The Poet As Politician," *Princeton Alumni Weekly*, November 3, 2010.

3. Herb Yazzie, "What Is a Nation?" (Fourth Annual William C. Canby Jr. Lecture, Sandra Day O'Connor College of Law, Arizona State University, January 27, 2011).

4. Brian W. Dippie, *The Vanishing American: White Attitudes and U.S. Indian Policy* (Middletown, CT: Wesleyan University Press, 1982).

5. Peterson Zah, "We Are Finally Growing Our Own" (presentation, Heard Museum, March 2010).

For Further Reading

Chapter 1. Generations

Bailey, Garrick, and Roberta Glenn Bailey. *A History of the Navajos: The Reservation Years.* Santa Fe, NM: School of American Research Press, 1986.

Begay, Shonto. *Navajo Visions and Voices across the Mesas.* New York: Scholastic, 1995.

Campbell, Tyrone, and Joel and Kate Kopp. *Navajo Pictorial Weaving, 1880–1950: Folk Art Images of Native Americans.* New York: Dutton Studio Books, 1991.

Cruikshank, Julie. *The Social Life of Stories: Narrative and Knowledge in the Yukon Territory.* Lincoln: University of Nebraska Press, 1998.

Cruikshank, Julie, with the collaboration of Angela Sidney, Kitty Smith, and Annie Ned. *Life Lived Like a Story: Life Stories of Three Yukon Native Elders.* Lincoln: University of Nebraska Press, 1990.

Deyhle, Donna. *Reflections in Place: Connected Lives of Navajo Women.* Tucson: University of Arizona Press, 2009.

Hartman, Russell, and Jan Musial. *Navajo Pottery: Tradition and Innovation.* Flagstaff, AZ: Northland Publishing, 1987.

Hedlund, Ann Lane. *Navajo Weaving in the Late Twentieth Century: Kin, Community, and Collectors.* Tucson: University of Arizona Press, 2004.

Holiday, John, and Robert McPherson. *A Navajo Legacy: The Life and Teachings of John Holiday.* Norman: University of Oklahoma Press, 2005.

Iverson, Peter. *Diné: A History of the Navajos.* Albuquerque: University of New Mexico Press, 2002.

Kelley, Klara Bonsack. *Navajo Land Usage: An Ethnoarchaeological Study.* Orlando, FL: Academic Press, 1988.

———, and Harris Francis. *Navajo Sacred Places.* Bloomington: Indiana University Press, 1994.

Lamphere, Louise, with Eva Price, Carole Cadman, and Valerie Darwin. *Weaving Women's Lives: Three Generations in a Navajo Family.* Albuquerque: University of New Mexico Press, 2007.

175

McCloskey, Joanne. *Living through the Generations: Community and Culture in Navajo Women's Lives.* Tucson: University of Arizona Press, 2007.

McPherson, Robert. *Navajo Land, Navajo Culture: The Utah Experience in the Twentieth Century.* Norman: University of Oklahoma Press, 2001.

Mitchell, Rose. *Tall Woman: The Life Story of Rose Mitchell, a Navajo Woman.* Ed. Charlotte J. Frisbie. Albuquerque: University of New Mexico Press, 2001.

Reid, Betty. *Navajo Women: Sáanii.* Photographs by Kenji Kuwano. Tucson, AZ: Rio Nuevo Publishers, 2007.

Rodee, Marian E. *One Hundred Years of Navajo Rugs.* Albuquerque: University of New Mexico Press, 1995.

Roessel, Monty. *Kinaaldá: A Navajo Girl Grows Up.* Minneapolis, MN: Lerner Publishing Group, 1993.

———. *Songs from the Loom: A Navajo Girl Learns to Weave.* Minneapolis, MN: Lerner Publishing Group, 1995.

Roessel, Ruth, ed. *Women in Navajo Society.* Chinle, AZ: Navajo Resources Center, Rough Rock Demonstration School, 1982.

Rosier, Paul C. *Serving Their County: American Indian Politics and Patriotism in the Twentieth Century.* Cambridge, MA: Harvard University Press, 2009.

Schweitzer, Marjorie M., ed. *American Indian Grandmothers: Traditions and Transitions.* Albuquerque: University of New Mexico Press, 1999.

Tapahonso, Luci. *Sáanii Dahataal/The Women Are Singing.* Tucson: University of Arizona Press, 1993.

———. *Blue Horses Rush In: Poems and Stories.* Tucson: University of Arizona Press, 1997.

———. *Songs of Shiprock Fair.* Illustrations by Anthony Chee Emerson. Walnut, CA: Kiva Publishing, 1999.

Towner, Ronald H., ed. *The Archaeology of Navajo Origins.* Salt Lake City: University of Utah Press, 1996.

Willink, RoseAnn S., and Paul Zolbrod. *Weaving a World: Textiles and the Navajo Way of Seeing.* Santa Fe: Museum of New Mexico Press, 1996.

Witherspoon, Gary. *Navajo Kinship and Marriage.* Chicago: University of Chicago Press, 1975.

Chapter 2. Schools

Adams, David Wallace. *Education for Extinction: American Indians and the Boarding School Experience.* Lawrence: University Press of Kansas, 1995.

Amerman, Stephen Kent. *Urban Indians in Phoenix Schools, 1940–2000.* Lincoln: University of Nebraska Press, 2010.

Archuleta, Margaret, Brenda Child, and K. Tsianina Lomawaima, eds. *Away from Home: Boarding School Experiences.* Phoenix, AZ: Heard Museum, 2001.

Benally, AnCita, ed. *A Handbook for Teachers of Navajo Children.* Tempe: Center for Indian Education, Arizona State University, 2005.

Child, Brenda. *Boarding School Seasons: American Indian Families, 1900–1940.* Lincoln: University of Nebraska Press, 1998.

Connell-Szasz, Margaret. *Education and the American Indian: The Road to Self-Determination since 1928.* 3rd ed. Albuquerque: University of New Mexico Press, 2000.

Coombs, L. Madison. *Doorway toward the Light: The Story of the Special Navajo Education Program.* Brigham City, UT: Bureau of Indian Affairs, 1954.

Doty, C. Stewart, Dale Sperry Mudge, and Herbert John Benally, eds. *Photographing Navajos: John Collier Jr. on the Reservation, 1948–1953.* Albuquerque: University of New Mexico Press, 2002.

Gilbert, Matthew Sakiestewa. *Education beyond the Mesas: Hopi Students at Sherman Institute, 1902–1929.* Lincoln: University of Nebraska Press, 2010.

Greenberg, Henry, and Georgia Greenberg. *Carl Gorman's World.* Albuquerque: University of New Mexico Press, 1984.

Hyer, Sally. *One House, One Voice, One Heart: The History of the Santa Fe Indian School.* Santa Fe: Museum of New Mexico Press, 1990.

Johnson, Broderick. *Navaho Education at Rough Rock.* Chinle, AZ: Rough Rock Demonstration School, 1968.

Lomawaima, K. Tsianina. *They Called It Prairie Light: A History of the Chilocco Indian School.* Lincoln: University of Nebraska Press, 1994.

Riney, Scott. *The Rapid City Indian School, 1898–1933.* Norman: University of Oklahoma Press, 1998.

Roessel, Robert A. *Indian Communities in Action.* Tempe: Arizona State University, 1967.

———. *Navajo Education, 1948–1978: Its Progress and Problems.* Chinle, AZ: Rough Rock Demonstration School, 1978.

Thompson, Hildegard. *The Navajos' Long Walk for Education.* Tsaile, AZ: Navajo Community College Press, 1975.

Trennert, Robert A. Jr. *The Phoenix Indian School: Enforced Acculturation in Arizona, 1891–1935.* Norman: University of Oklahoma Press, 1988.

Young, Robert W. *The Navajo Yearbook, 1951–1961.* Window Rock, AZ: Bureau of Indian Affairs, 1961.

Chapter 3. Leaders

Blaine, Peter Sr., with Michael S. Adams. *Papagos and Politics.* Tucson: Arizona Historical Society, 1981.

Connell-Szasz, Margaret, ed. *Between Indian and White Worlds: The Cultural Broker.* Norman: University of Oklahoma Press, 1994.

Denetdale, Jennifer Nez. *Reclaiming Diné History: The Legacy of Navajo Chief Manuelito and Juanita.* Tucson: University of Arizona Press, 2007.

Edmunds, R. David, ed. *Native American Leaders: Studies in Diversity.* Lincoln: University of Nebraska Press, 1980.

——, ed. *The New Warriors: Native American Leaders since 1900.* Lincoln: University of Nebraska Press, 2001.

Frisbie, Charlotte J., and David P. McAllister, eds. *Navajo Blessingway Singer: The Autobiography of Frank Mitchell, 1881–1967.* Tucson: University of Arizona Press, 1978.

Hoffman, Virginia, and Broderick Johnson. *Navajo Biographies.* Chinle, AZ: Rough Rock Demonstration School, 1970.

Iverson, Peter. *Carlos Montezuma and the Changing World of American Indians.* Albuquerque: University of New Mexico Press, 1982.

——. *The Navajo Nation.* Albuquerque: University of New Mexico Press, 1983.

——, ed. *"For Our Navajo People": Diné Letters, Speeches & Petitions, 1900–1960.* Albuquerque: University of New Mexico Press, 2002.

MacDonald, Peter, with Ted Schwarz. *The Last Warrior: Peter MacDonald and the Navajo Nation.* New York: Orion Books, 1993.

Moses, L. G., and Raymond Wilson, eds. *Indian Lives: Essays in Nineteenth- and Twentieth-Century Native American Life.* Lawrence: University Press of Kansas, 1993.

Niethammer, Carolyn. *"I'll Go and Do More": Annie Dodge Wauneka, Navajo Leader and Activist.* Lincoln: University of Nebraska Press, 2001.

Parman, Donald. *The Navajos and the New Deal.* New Haven, CT: Yale University Press, 1976.

Shepardson, Mary. *Navajo Ways in Government: A Study in Political Process.* Menasha, WI: American Anthropological Association, 1963.

Shreve, Bradley C. *Red Power Rising: The National Indian Youth Council and the Origins of Nation Activism.* Norman: University of Oklahoma Press, 2011.

Stewart, Irene. *A Voice in Her Tribe: A Navajo Woman's Own Story.* Socorro, NM: Ballena Press, 1980.

Wilkinson, Charles. *Blood Struggle: The Rise of Modern Indian Nations.* New York: W. W. Norton, 2005.

Chapter 4. Lawyers

Bingham, Sam, and Janet Bingham, eds. *Navajo Chapters.* Tsaile, AZ: Navajo Community College Press, 1997.

Fixico, Donald. *Termination and Relocation: Federal Indian Policy, 1945–1960.* Albuquerque: University of New Mexico Press, 1976.

Kelly, Lawrence C. *The Navajo Indians and Federal Policy, 1900–1935.* Tucson: University of Arizona Press, 1968.

———. *The Assault on Assimilation: John Collier and the Origins of Indian Policy Reform.* Albuquerque: University of New Mexico Press, 1983.

Maroukis, Thomas C. *The Peyote Road: Religious Freedom and the Native American Church.* Norman: University of Oklahoma Press, 2010.

McDonald, Laughlin. *American Indians and the Fight for Equal Voting Rights.* Norman: University of Oklahoma Press, 2010.

McMillen, Christian W. *Making Indian Law: The Hualapai Land Case and the Birth of Ethnohistory.* New Haven: Yale University Press, 2010.

Moore, Lucy. *Into the Canyon: Seven Years in Navajo Country.* Albuquerque: University of New Mexico Press, 2004.

Nielsen, Marianne O., and James W. Zion, eds. *Navajo Nation Peacemaking: Living Traditional Justice.* Tucson: University of Arizona Press, 2005.

Philp, Kenneth. *John Collier's Crusade for Indian Reform, 1920–1954.* Tucson: University of Arizona Press, 1977.

———. *Termination Revisited: American Indians on the Road to Self-Determination, 1933–1953.* Lincoln: University of Nebraska Press, 1999.

Pommersheim, Frank. *Broken Landscapes: Indians, Indian Tribes, and the Constitution.* New York: Oxford University Press, 2009.

Wilkins, David E. *The Navajo Political Experience.* Tsaile, AZ: Diné College Press, 1999.

———, and K. Tsianina Lomawaima. *Uneven Ground: American Indian Sovereignty and Federal Law.* Norman: University of Oklahoma Press, 2005.

Wilkinson, Charles. *Fire on the Plateau: Conflict and Endurance in the American Southwest.* Washington, D.C.: Island Press, 2004.

———. *Blood Struggle: The Rise of Modern Indian Nations.* New York: W. W. Norton, 2005.

Williams, Aubrey. *Navajo Political Process.* Washington, D.C.: Smithsonian Institution Press, 1980.

Work, L. Susan. *The Seminole Nation of Oklahoma: A Legal History.* Norman: University of Oklahoma Press, 2010.

Young, Robert W. *A Political History of the Navajo Tribe.* Tsaile, AZ: Navajo Community College Press, 1978.

Chapter 5. Traders

Adair, John. *The Navajo and Pueblo Silversmiths.* Norman: University of Oklahoma Press, 1944.

Adams, William Y. *Shonto: A Study of the Role of the Trader in a Modern Navajo Community.* Smithsonian Institution, Bureau of American Ethnology, Bulletin 188. Washington, D.C.: Government Printing Office, 1963.

Batkin, Jonathan. *The Native American Curio Trade in New Mexico.* Santa Fe, NM: Wheelwright Museum of the American Indian, 2008.

Berkowitz, Paul. *The Case of the Indian Trader: Billy Malone and the National Park Service Investigation at Hubbell Trading Post.* Albuquerque: University of New Mexico Press, 2011.

Blue, Martha. *Indian Trader: The Life and Times of J. L. Hubbell.* Walnut, CA: Kiva Publishing, 2000.

Brugge, David M. *Hubbell Trading Post National Historic Site.* Tucson, AZ: Southwest Parks and Monuments Association, 1993.

Cousins, Jean, and Bill Cousins. *Tales from Wide Ruins.* Lubbock: Texas Tech University Press, 1996.

Gillmore, Frances, and Louisa Wade Wetherill. *Traders to the Navaho.* Albuquerque: University of New Mexico Press, 1934.

Graves, Laura. *Thomas Varker Keam: Indian Trader.* Norman: University of Oklahoma Press, 1998.

Hall, Edward T. *West of the Thirties: Discoveries among the Navajo and Hopi.* New York: Doubleday, 1994.

Hegemann, Elizabeth C. *Navaho Trading Days.* Albuquerque: University of New Mexico Press, 1963.

Howard, Kathleen, and Diana Pardue, eds. *Inventing the Southwest: The Fred Harvey Company and Native American Art.* Flagstaff, AZ: Northland Publishing, 1998.

James, H. L. *Rugs and Posts: The Story of Navajo Weaving and Indian Trading.* West Chester, PA: Schiffer Publishing, 1988.

M'Closkey, Kathy. *Swept under the Rug: The Hidden History of Navajo Weaving.* Albuquerque: University of New Mexico Press, 2002.

McNitt, Frank. *The Indian Traders.* Norman: University of Oklahoma Press, 1961.

Moon, Samuel. *Tall Sheep: Harry Goulding, Monument Valley Trader.* Norman: University of Oklahoma Press, 1992.

Powers, Willow Roberts. *Navajo Trading: The End of an Era.* Albuquerque: University of New Mexico Press, 2001.

Richardson, Gladwell. *Navajo Trader.* Tucson: University of Arizona Press, 1982.

Roberts, Willow. *Stokes Carson: Twentieth-Century Trading on the Navajo Reservation.* Albuquerque: University of New Mexico Press, 1987.

Wagner, Sallie Lippincott. *Wide Ruins: Memories from a Navajo Trading Post.* Albuquerque: University of New Mexico Press, 1997.

Wheat, Joe Ben. *Blanket Weaving in the Southwest.* Ed. Ann Lane Hedlund. Tucson: University of Arizona Press, 2003.

Whitaker, Kathleen. *Southwest Textiles: Weavings of the Navajo and Pueblo.* Seattle: University of Washington Press; Los Angeles: Southwest Museum, 2002.

Chapter 6. Neighbors

Basso, Keith H. *Wisdom Sits in Places: Landscape and Language among the Western Apaches.* Albuquerque: University of New Mexico Press, 1996.

Benally, Malcolm D., ed. and trans. *Bitter Water: Diné Oral Histories of the Navajo–Hopi Land Dispute.* Tucson: University of Arizona Press, 2011.

Benedek, Emily. *The Wind Won't Know Me: A History of the Navajo–Hopi Land Dispute.* New York: Knopf, 1992.

Brugge, David. *The Navajo–Hopi Land Dispute: An American Tragedy.* Albuquerque: University of New Mexico Press, 1980.

Clemmer, Richard O. *Roads in the Sky: The Hopi Indians in a Century of Change.* Boulder, CO: Westview Press, 1995.

Dillingham, Rick. *Fourteen Families in Pueblo Pottery.* Albuquerque: University of New Mexico Press, 1994.

Fisher, Nora. *Rio Grande Textiles.* Santa Fe: Museum of New Mexico Press, 1994.

Griffin-Pierce, Trudy. *Native Peoples of the Southwest.* Albuquerque: University of New Mexico Press, 2000.

———. *The Columbia Guide to the American Indians of the Southwest.* New York: Columbia University Press, 2010.

Hebner, William Logan. *Southern Paiute: A Portrait.* Logan: Utah State University Press, 2011.

Heth, Charlotte, ed. *Native American Dance: Ceremonies and Social Traditions.* Washington, D.C.: National Museum of the American Indian, 1997.

Hucko, Bruce, and the Voices of the Children of Santa Clara, San Ildefonso, San Juan, Pojoaque, and Nambe Pueblos. *Where There Is No Name for Art: The Art of Tewa Pueblo Children.* Santa Fe, NM: School of American Research Press, 1996.

Hughtie, Phil. *A Zuni Artist Looks at Frank Hamilton Cushing.* Zuni, NM: Pueblo of Zuni Arts and Crafts A:Shiwi A:Wan Museum and Heritage Center, 1994.

Kammer, Jerry. *The Second Long Walk: The Navajo–Hopi Land Dispute.* Albuquerque: University of New Mexico Press, 1980.

Knack, Martha C. *Boundaries Between: The Southern Paiutes, 1775–1975.* Lincoln: University of Nebraska Press, 2002.

Laird, W. David. *Hopi Bibliography.* Tucson: University of Arizona Press, 1977.

Levo-Henriksson, Ritva. *Media and Ethnic Identity: Hopi Views on Media, Identity, and Communication.* New York: Routledge, 2007.

Marmon, Lee. *The Pueblo Imagination: Landscape and Memory in the Photography of Lee Marmon.* Boston: Beacon Press, 2003.

Meeks, Eric. *Border Citizens: The Making of Indians, Mexicans, and Anglos in Arizona.* Austin: University of Texas Press, 2007.

Ortiz, Alfonso, ed. *Southwest.* Vol. 9 of *Handbook of North American Indians.* Washington, D.C.: Smithsonian Institution, 1979.

———, ed. *Southwest.* Vol. 10 of *Handbook of North American Indians.* Washington, D.C.: Smithsonian Institution, 1983.

Ortiz, Simon. *Woven Stone.* Tucson: University of Arizona Press, 1992.

Scott, Jay. *Changing Woman: The Life and Art of Helen Hardin.* Flagstaff, AZ: Northland Publishing, 1989.

Shepherd, Jeffrey P. *We Are an Indian Nation: A History of the Hualapai People.* Tucson: University of Arizona Press, 2010.

Sheridan, Thomas E., and Nancy J. Parezo, eds. *Paths of Life: American Indians of the Southwest and Northern Mexico.* Tucson: University of Arizona Press, 1986.

Spicer, Edward H. *Cycles of Conquest: The Impact of Spain, Mexico, and the United States on the Indians of the Southwest, 1533–1960.* Tucson: University of Arizona Press, 1961.

Teiwes, Helga. *Hopi Basket Weaving: Artistry in Natural Fibers.* Tucson: University of Arizona Press, 1996.

Trimble, Stephen. *The People: Indians of the American Southwest.* Santa Fe, NM: School of American Research Press, 1993.

Vincenti Carpio, Myla. *Indigenous Albuquerque.* Lubbock: Texas Tech University Press, 2011.

Weaver, Thomas, ed. *Indians of Arizona: A Contemporary Perspective.* Tucson: University of Arizona Press, 1974.

Wenger, Tisa. *We Have a Religion: The 1920s Pueblo Indian Dance Controversy and American Religious Freedom.* Chapel Hill: University of North Carolina Press, 2009.

Whiteford, Andrew. *Southwestern Indian Baskets: Their History and Their Makers.* Santa Fe, NM: School of American Research Press, 1988.

Whitely, Peter. *Deliberate Acts: Changing Hopi Culture through the Oraibi Split.* Tucson: University of Arizona Press, 1987.

Wyckoff, Lydia L., ed. *Visions and Voices: Native American Painting from the Philbrook Museum of Art.* Tulsa, OK: Philbrook Museum of Art, 1996.

Chapter 7. Resources

Ambler, Marjane. *Breaking the Iron Bonds: Indian Control of Energy Development.* Lawrence: University Press of Kansas, 1990.

Baars, Donald L. *Navajo Country: A Geology and Natural History of the Four Corners Region.* Albuquerque: University of New Mexico Press, 1985.

Bingham, Sam, and Janet Bingham, eds. *Navajo Farming.* Rock Point, AZ: Rock Point Community School, 1979.

———. *Between Sacred Mountains: Navajo Stories and Lessons from the Land.* Tucson: Sun Tracks and the University of Arizona Press, 1984.

Boyce, George. *When the Navajos Had Too Many Sheep: The 1940s.* San Francisco: Indian Historian Press, 1974.

Brugge, David M. *A History of the Chaco Navajos.* Albuquerque, NM: National Park Service, 1979.

Brugge, Doug, Timothy Benally, and Esther Yazzie-Lewis, eds. *The Navajo People and Uranium Mining.* Albuquerque: University of New Mexico Press, 2006.

Chamberlain, Kathleen. *Under Sacred Ground: A History of Navajo Oil.* Albuquerque: University of New Mexico Press, 2000.

Downs, James. *Animal Husbandry in Navajo Society and Culture.* Berkeley: University of California Press, 1964.

Fixico, Donald. *The Invasion of Indian Country in the Twentieth Century: American Capitalism and Tribal Natural Resources.* Niwot: University Press of Colorado, 1998.

Fradkin, Philip L. *A River No More: The Colorado River and the West.* New York: Knopf, 1981.

Goodman, James M. *The Navajo Atlas: Environments, Resources, People and History of the Diné Bikéyah.* Norman: University of Oklahoma Press, 1982.

Iverson, Peter. *When Indians Became Cowboys: Native Peoples and Cattle Ranching in the American West.* Norman: University of Oklahoma Press, 1994.

McCool, Daniel. *Native Waters: Contemporary Indian Water Settlements and the Second Treaty Era.* Tucson: University of Arizona Press, 2002.

McPherson, Robert S. *Comb Ridge and Its People: The Ethnohistory of a Rock.* Logan: Utah State University Press, 2009.

O'Neill, Colleen. *Working the Navajo Way: Labor and Culture in the Twentieth Century.* Lawrence: University Press of Kansas, 2005.

Reno, Philip. *Mother Earth, Father Sky, and Economic Development: Navajo Resources and Their Use.* Albuquerque: University of New Mexico Press, 1981.

Sherry, John W. *Land, Wind, and Hard Words: A Story of Navajo Activism.* Albuquerque: University of New Mexico Press, 2002.

Weisiger, Marsha. *Dreaming of Sheep in Navajo Country.* Seattle: University of Washington Press, 2009.

White, Richard. *The Roots of Dependency: Subsistence, Economy, and Social Change among the Choctaws, Pawnees, and Navajos.* Lincoln: University of Nebraska Press, 1981.

Youngdahl, Jay. *Working on the Railroad, Walking in Beauty: Navajos, Hózhó, and Track Work.* Logan: Utah State University Press, 2011.

Chapter 8. Tomorrows

Davies, Wade M. *Healing Ways: Navajo Health Care in the Twentieth Century.* Albuquerque: University of New Mexico Press, 2000.

Emerson, Gloria J. *At the Helm of the Lowest Clouds: Meditations on Navajo Landscapes.* Santa Fe, NM: School of American Research Press, 2003.

Frisbie, Charlotte J. *Navajo Medicine Bundles or Jish: Acquisition, Transmission, and Disposition in the Past and Present.* Albuquerque: University of New Mexico Press, 1997.

House, Deborah. *Language Shift among the Navajo: Identity Politics and Cultural Continuity.* Tucson: University of Arizona Press, 2002.

Hurtado, Albert, ed. *Reflections on American Indian History: Honoring the Past, Building a Future.* Norman: University of Oklahoma Press, 2008.

Iverson, Peter. *"We Are Still Here": American Indians in the Twentieth Century.* Wheeling, IL: Harlan Davidson, 1998.

———. *Riders of the West: Portraits from Indian Rodeo.* Photographs by Linda MacCannell. Seattle: University of Washington Press, 1999.

Kristovic, Jim. *Navajos Wear Nikes: A Reservation Life.* Albuquerque: University of New Mexico Press, 2011.

McCullough-Brabson, Ellen, and Marilyn Help. *We'll Be in Your Mountains, We'll Be in Your Songs: A Navajo Woman Sings.* Albuquerque: University of New Mexico Press, 2001.

Meeks, Barbra A. *We Are Our Language: An Ethnography of Language Revitalization in a Northern Athabascan Community.* Tucson: University of Arizona Press, 2011.

Pardue, Diana, with the Heard Museum. *Contemporary Southwestern Jewelry.* Layton, UT: Gibbs Smith Publisher, 2007.

Rosenak, Chuck, and Jan Rosenak. *Navajo Folk Art.* 2nd ed. Tucson: Rio Nuevo Publishers, 2008.

Wilkinson, Charles. *The People Are Dancing Again: The History of the Siletz Tribe of Western Oregon.* Seattle: University of Washington Press, 2010.

Illustration Credits

Frontispiece. Portrait of Peterson Zah. Unknown photographer; Special Collections, Hayden Library, Arizona State University. LAB MSS 154:67/5.39.

The San Francisco Peaks (page 15). Photograph by Edward J. Dawson; Special Collections, Cline Library, Northern Arizona University. NAU. PH.2006.41.6.56.

Navajo sheep mingle in the Tuba City area (page 17). Photograph by Mary May Bailey, 1928; Special Collections, Cline Library, Northern Arizona University. NAU.PH.99.54.285.

A Navajo family shears a sheep (page 20). Photograph by Josef Muench; Special Collections, Cline Library, Northern Arizona University. NAU. PH.2003.11.3.E8552.

A Navajo girl learning to weave (page 22). Photograph by Milton Snow, 1941; Special Collections, Hayden Library, Arizona State University. CP SPC 168:3.

Shonto sheep and boy (page 23). Photograph by Philip Johnston, 1932; Special Collections, Cline Library, Northern Arizona University. NAU. PH.413.675.

The community of Keams Canyon (page 28). Photograph by Milton Snow, 1944; Special Collections, Cline Library, Northern Arizona University. HCPO.PH.2003.1.HE1.4.

Playground at Keams Canyon Boarding School (page 29). Photograph by Milton Snow, 1945; Special Collections, Cline Library, Northern Arizona University. HCPO.PH. 2003.1.HF1.17.

A Navajo girl irons in a home economics class at Keams Canyon Boarding School (page 30). Photograph by Milton Snow, 1944; Special Collections, Cline Library, Northern Arizona University. HCPO.PH.2003.1.HF1.6.

A young Navajo boy takes on a new environment (page 32). Unknown photographer, 1955; Special Collections, Cline Library, Northern Arizona University. NAU.PH.92.14.81.

Navajo field (page 34). Photograph by Milton Snow, 1941; Special Collections, Hayden Library, Arizona State University.

Students at the Tuba City Boarding School (page 37). Unknown photographer, 1956; Special Collections, Cline Library, Northern Arizona University. NAU.ARC.1956/57-15-5.

Henry Chee Dodge (page 49). Photograph by Leo Crane, 1934; Special Collections, Cline Library, Northern Arizona University. NAU. PH.658.995.

Horse reduction (page 53). Photograph by Milton Snow, 1940; Arizona Historical Foundation.

Annie Wauneka with her colleagues on the Navajo Tribal Council (page 56). Unknown photographer; Leslie Goodluck Collection, Special Collections, Cline Library, Northern Arizona University. NAU.PH.2003.13.4.4.

Raymond Nakai (page 65). Unknown photographer, 1961; Raymond Nakai Collection, Special Collections, Cline Library, Northern Arizona University. NAU.PH.2006.16.1.2.15.

Campaign for Raymond Nakai (page 65). Unknown photographer; Special Collections, Cline Library, Northern Arizona University. NAU. PH.2006.16.2.82.

Exterior view of the Navajo Tribal Council chambers (page 69). Photograph by Josef Muench; Special Collections, Cline Library, Northern Arizona University. NAU.PH.2003.11.10.9.E8165.

Interior view of the Navajo Tribal Council chambers (page 71). Photograph by Josef Muench; Special Collections, Cline Library, Northern Arizona University. NAU.PH.2003.11.10.9.E 8159.

Peterson Zah at DNA People's Legal Services Program meeting (page 74). Unknown photographer; Special Collections, Hayden Library, Arizona State University. LAB MSS 154:67/6.1.

Raymond Nakai and Peter MacDonald (page 94). Unknown photographer; Special Collections, Cline Library, Northern Arizona University. NAU.PH.2006.16.2.123.

Shonto Trading Post (page 98). Photograph by Tad Nichols; Special Collections, Cline Library, Northern Arizona University. NAU.PH.99.3.7.3.1.

Navajo wagon (page 100). Photograph by Milton Snow, 1940. Kéyah tse kohi'; Special Collections, Hayden Library, Arizona State University. CP SPC 168:5.

Truck at Lukachukai Trading Post (page 100). Unknown photographer, 1947; Troy and Edith Kennedy Collection, Special Collections, Cline Library, Northern Arizona University. NAU.PH.98.71.3.

Tocito Trading Post (page 101). Unknown photographer, 1955; Grace and Charles Herring Collection, Special Collections, Cline Library, Northern Arizona University. NAU.PH.98.21.27.

Ivan Sidney, Peterson Zah, and Harry Kinney, the mayor of Albuquerque (page 112). Special Collections, Hayden Library, Arizona State University. LAB MSS 154:64/7.2.

Inauguration ceremonies for Peterson Zah as chairman of the Navajo Tribal Council (page 115). Unknown photographer, 1983; Special Collections, Hayden Library, Arizona State University. LAB MSS 154:64/7.19.

Peterson Zah and Louis Denetsosie (page 117). Unknown photographer; Special Collections, Hayden Library, Arizona State University. LAB MSS 154:64/6.4.

Hopi sheep (page 119). Photograph by Milton Snow, 1944; Special Collections, Cline Library, Northern Arizona University. HCPO.PH.2003 .1.HM5.5.

Hopis and Navajos playing basketball (page 119). Photograph by Milton Snow, 1944; Special Collections, Cline Library, Northern Arizona University. HCPO.PH.2003.1.HF5.14.

Canyon de Chelly and Black Mesa (page 121). Photograph by Milton Snow, 1940; Special Collections, Hayden Library, Arizona State University. LAB MSS 154:64/6.4.

A Navajo Forest Products Industry truck moving lumber (page 124). Photograph by Josef Muench, 1950–1970; Special Collections, Cline Library, Northern Arizona University. NAU.PH.2003.11.10.8.H298.

Navajo employees sort lumber at the Navajo Forest Products Industry facility (page 125). Photograph by Josef Muench, 1950–1970; Special Collections, Cline Library, Northern Arizona University. NAU.PH.2003 .11.10.8.H307.

Jeeps move tourists through Canyon de Chelly (page 126). Photograph by Tad Nichols, 1958; Special Collections, Cline Library, Northern Arizona University. NAU.PH.99.3.7.6.23.

Kayenta, Arizona (page 126). Photograph by Josef Muench 1950–1970; Special Collections, Cline Library, Northern Arizona University. NAU.PH. 2003.11.10.9.H1182.

Monument Valley at sunrise (page 128). Photograph by Josef Muench, 1950–1970; Special Collections, Cline Library, Northern Arizona University. NAU.PH.2003.11.3.4880.

Peterson Zah meets with students (page 156). Unknown photographer; Special Collections, Hayden Library, Arizona State University. LAB MSS 154:65/2.13.

Peterson Zah is awarded an honorary degree (page 162). Photograph by Tim Trimble, Arizona State University.

Spider Rock in Canyon de Chelly (page 163). Photograph by Edward J. Dawson; Special Collections, Cline Library, Northern Arizona University. NAU.PH.2006.41.6.34.

Aspens with San Francisco Peaks in the distance (page 168). Photograph by Josef Muench; Special Collections, Cline Library, Northern Arizona University. NAU.PH.2003.11.7.3.A6037.

Map 1. Four Corners Area (page 9). (From Iverson, Peter, *Diné: A History of the Navajos* [Albuquerque: University of New Mexico Press, 2002])

Map 2. The Navajo Nation Today (page 10). (From Iverson, Peter, *Diné: A History of the Navajos* [Albuquerque: University of New Mexico Press, 2002])

Index

About the Authors

BORN IN KEAMS CANYON, ARIZONA, in 1937, Peterson Zah has long been a major figure in Navajo and Southwestern life. He has exemplified the determination of Indian people to gain greater control over their lives and lands. Zah became well known throughout the Navajo Nation and the surrounding region as the director of the DNA People's Legal Services program. The Navajos later elected him as chairman of the Navajo Tribal Council and as president of the Navajo Nation. For the past fifteen years, he served as a special advisor to the Arizona State University (ASU) president in regard to Indian issues and concerns. In 2005, ASU awarded him an honorary doctorate.

Zah's interest in education is rooted in personal experience. He was one of a handful of Navajo students of his generation who completed successfully the long journey to obtain a college degree. It has given him great satisfaction to be in a position to assist students to finish their studies. He applauds the kind of investment the Navajo Nation has made in the education of its young people. He sees it as a vital action necessary to secure the Navajo future.

PETER IVERSON IS REGENTS' PROFESSOR of History (Emeritus) at Arizona State University (ASU). He is the author or editor of fifteen books, including *Diné: A History of the Navajos*, *"For Our Navajo People": Diné Letters, Speeches & Petitions, 1900–1960*, *The Navajo Nation*, and *"We Are Still Here": American Indians in the Twentieth Century*.

His work has been supported by research fellowships from the Guggenheim Foundation, the National Endowment for the Humanities, and the Newberry Library. Iverson received his BA

from Carleton College and his MA and PhD from the University of Wisconsin–Madison.

He taught at Navajo Community College (now Diné College) during its first years and at ASU from 1986 to 2010. During his years at ASU, he also directed forty-eight PhD students to the completion of their dissertations. He has served as president of the Western History Association and has been given awards for his service to the Ak-Chin Indian Community and the Navajo Nation.